anoS

THE BOOK

By BRETT MARTIN

Designed by HEADCASE DESIGN

Produced by   Published by

HBO
IT'S NOT TV. IT'S HBO™

MELCHER MEDIA

Time Inc.
HOME ENTERTAINMENT

ISBN 13: 978-1-933821-87-0
ISBN 10:   1-933821-87-6

First printing,
May 2007

10 9 8 7 6 5 4 3 2 1

Printed in China

THE SOPRANOS

THE BOOK

"WE'RE JUST LIKE ANY OTHER FAMILY."

—TONY SOPRANO

THE Sopr

CHAPTER 1

"WOKE UP TH

IS MORNING"

THE BIRTH OF A SHOW

HERE'S THE THING:

IT WAS NEVER SUPPOSED TO WORK.

NOT A CHANCE. NOBODY THOUGHT SO. NOT THE ACTORS, THE PRODUCERS, THE NETWORK, NOT EVEN THE MAN FROM WHOSE BRAIN *THE SOPRANOS* SPRANG TO LIFE.

In the beginning, the show that was about to become a national phenomenon and would change the way people watched, thought, and talked about television seemed like a very bad idea indeed.

In fact, the earliest seed of the show probably *was* a bad idea. "I was standing by the elevators at the offices of Brillstein-Grey, my agency, and somebody casually asked if I was interested in producing a television version of *The Godfather*," says series creator David Chase. "It was a terrible idea. Just horrible," says Brad Grey, who remains an executive producer of *The Sopranos*, and is now chairman and CEO of Paramount Pictures. "Luckily, David immediately recognized it as such."

THIS WAS 1995 AND CHASE, THEN FIFTY years old, was already a television veteran, having been a writer/producer of *The Rockford Files* for several years, and executive producer of *Northern Exposure* and the series *I'll Fly Away*. It was a career to be proud of, complete with a handful of Emmys®, Peabodys, and other awards. When it came to running an hour-long dramatic show he was considered one of the best in the business, and his writing prowess had been honored with an Emmy® for the 1980 TV movie *Off the Minnesota Strip*. But Chase, a devotee of such film auteurs as Kubrick, Scorsese, and Polanski, was unhappy working in television. "Frankly, I did a bad thing," he said, as recently as the third season of *The Sopranos*. "I took the money. I didn't have the guts to stop it and I compromised."

Not that two decades in television had failed to teach Chase some valuable lessons. In particular, *Rockford*—starring James Garner as a laconic, muscle-car-driving private eye who just wants to stay out of trouble—had driven home the joys to be found in toying with a venerable genre. "Rockford was TV's first postmodern, ironic detective," Chase says. "He took all of the private eye clichés, dismantled and then reassembled them." *Rockford* creator Stephen J. Cannell imparted a crucial maxim for getting away with such

Above and previous spread: Series creator David Chase

imagined Robert De Niro and Anne Bancroft playing the main roles." (As it happened, at around the same time De Niro did take a role as a mobster in therapy. He starred in Harold Ramis's feature comedy *Analyze This*. "When someone told me about it, I thought, *Oh, fuck*. It was incredible," Chase remembers. "But we wound up coming out first, so it was all right. Otherwise, it would have just seemed like another case of TV copying the movies.")

Chase began shopping the idea to TV networks. One executive, in a near parody of a Hollywood exchange, professed to love the idea but wondered if the main character (then named Tommy Soprano) really needed to be in therapy. (Chase's answer was "Yes.") Eventually, Fox ordered a pilot script, but Chase says he never even received a call from the network to say that they'd passed on the result. "Suddenly, after it was written, they discovered they didn't want a mob/family drama," he says.

Finally, out of other options, Chase's agents and Brad Grey arranged a pitch meeting with HBO, which was seeking to extend its budding reputation for original series, built with such shows as *The Larry Sanders Show, Sex and the City,* and *Oz*. According to HBO Entertainment president Carolyn Strauss, who was then vice president of original programming, it was easy to see that the script had

subversion, one Chase would keep in mind while creating his own, much darker, antihero: "Cannell taught me that Tony Soprano can do a lot of bad things and make all kinds of mistakes—just like Jim Rockford can be lazy and look like a fool—so long as he's always the smartest guy in the room and he's good at his job. That's what we ask of our heroes: They can be doctors, gun slingers, brutes, bullies, mob bosses, whatever—they'd just better be good at it."

GRAFTING THE TRAPPINGS OF A GANGSTER FILM ONTO A DOMESTIC DRAMA ... CREATED A CHARACTER WHO WAS BOTH UNIQUE AND ENTIRELY RECOGNIZABLE.

By the mid-nineties there was little question that Chase was good at what *he* did, and he had been rewarded by a succession of studio development deals and failed pilots. Still, he remained unsatisfied and it seemed certain that a small-screen version of *The Godfather* wasn't the answer. "I didn't want to do that because it had been done before," Chase says. On the drive home, however, an idea began to turn over in Chase's mind. For years, he had been telling friends, and a few therapists, stories of growing up with a difficult mother in suburban New Jersey. To write about the relationship directly, he'd always thought, would be self-indulgent. But he'd also had a lifelong interest in the workings of organized crime.

"I started to think about this feature film idea in which a New Jersey mobster was having trouble with his mother because he had put her in a nursing home instead of letting her live with him, which is the old Italian way of doing things. And he went to a therapist who would figure out, long before he did, that his mother was probably his enemy," Chase remembers. "It was sort of a comedy. I

promise. "Everybody could see that it was a good piece of material. The voice of the script was great. The characters were well-formed. David really knew what he wanted to do and why. The question was whether it was the right project for us," Strauss says. She and the other HBO executives worried about whether audiences would be willing to embrace a protagonist like Tony Soprano. "There was a lot of debate about whether people would respond to him," Strauss says.

Chase produced a rewrite of the script and waited. In the meantime, he had been offered yet another network development deal and was putting off signing until hearing HBO's decision. Finally, the other network would wait no longer; Chase was scheduled to sign the deal at 2 P.M. At noon, HBO called. "They said, 'We want to go ahead. We want to do it,'" Chase says. "I felt like I'd been let out of jail. It was like a reprieve from the governor."

By then, Chase had already begun to vaguely, possibly see the potential for the story to be more than a simple genre comedy. By grafting the trappings of a gangster film onto a domestic drama, all set in the end-of-millennium suburbs, Chase had created a character who was both unique and entirely recognizable. When Tony famously told Dr. Melfi, "Lately I feel like I came in at the end of something. The best is over," he might have specifically been talking about the downfall of the Mafia, but he could have been speaking for any number of baby-boomers who woke up one morning to find themselves with a good job, a beautiful house, a nice car, and a queer sense of emptiness. He might as well have been talking about the failings of the American dream.

Such acute monitoring of the national temperature has been a feature of *The Sopranos* throughout its run. The show has dealt with issues from gentrification to gay rights to the various ripple effects of September 11. The latter has been evoked both literally—when FBI

Agent Harris is transferred from the pork store beat to counter-terrorism work in Afghanistan—and more subtly in the ever-increasing sense of dislocation the characters seem to feel. It's hard to watch Tony resolve to change, only to revert to his old ways, without thinking of the countless resolutions of change made—and gradually forgotten—by many Americans in the wake of September 11. "That's thematic in the show," Chase says. "We all do it. I do it. We wake up and say, 'I have to do a better job of living my life. I have to be a better person. I have to do something.' And then, we don't."

FINDING TONY

"**W**E HAD A GREAT SCRIPT, ALL THE SCENES were working well on paper, but then it was like, Now we have to actually go out and find these people,'" says executive producer Ilene Landress.

First and foremost, of course, was the task of casting Tony Soprano. Many actors were in the running. Before HBO came in, while the pilot was still with Fox, Australian Anthony LaPaglia, who went on to star in network TV's *Without a Trace*, was considered for the role. At various points, Steven Van Zandt, and Michael Rispoli, who eventually took on the role of Jackie Aprile, were also in the running. It is no disrespect to any of these fine actors' talents to say that it is inconceivable to imagine anybody but James Gandolfini in the role. "Finding Jim was everything," Chase says, simply. "Without him, we never get on the air. Without him, the show doesn't exist."

"THIS WASN'T FOUR PRETTY WOMEN IN MANHATTAN."
— JAMES GANDOLFINI

Landress remembers holding auditions for the pilot in a tiny walk-up studio on W. 72nd Street in Manhattan, the sounds of a tap-dance rehearsal upstairs ringing through the floor. One day, she was told that a character actor named James Gandolfini was coming in to read for Tony. As it happened, she had heard of Gandolfini, who had played a number of bad guys and heavies on film and stage. "He had . . . something," Landress says. "He brought a weight to the scenes, a kind of gravity. It was clear that this was the guy."

That HBO would even consider casting a leading man with thinning hair, a somewhat bulging waistline, and a crooked smile was a welcome sign of commitment to making the show something different. "This wasn't four pretty women in Manhattan," Gandolfini says. "This was a bunch of fat guys from Jersey. It was an incredible leap of faith."

It was faith well rewarded. Gandolfini seemed to fully inhabit Tony Soprano almost immediately, sometimes in ways that surprised even the character's creator. "We shot the last scene of the pilot on the first day of shooting. It was the barbecue scene, where they were trying to cheer Artie Bucco up after his restaurant had burned down," Chase says. "Christopher was pissed off because he felt he hadn't gotten enough credit for the garbage contract thing and had said that maybe he was going to sell his story to Hollywood. In the script, it was written that Tony sort of slapped him and said, 'What are you, crazy?' But Jim fucking went nuts—picked him up and slammed him down. I thought, *Wow. Right. That's exactly right.*"

Gandolfini is more modest about his talents. "It wasn't that hard," he demurs. "I grew up ten minutes from where this show took place. I'm an Italian kid from Jersey. My family—while there's nobody in it like Livia Soprano—is a dark group. I'm from this world." A large part of what became Tony's character, he says, came simply from the intense strains of filming a show in which he appeared in almost every scene. "In the beginning, it was ridiculous. We were shooting sixteen- or seventeen-hour days and then I had to go home and memorize five or six more pages of dialogue," he says. "And it was brutal stuff: mothers trying to kill you and therapy scenes where you're talking for four pages with the camera right on your face. It was no joke. I used to call David in the middle of the night and scream at him: 'You're fucking killing me! I'll give the money back, just make it stop!'" He smiles: "Obviously, they didn't cast me in this part because I was such a normal, well-balanced human being."

"There's where your 'gravity' comes from," he says, laughing. "Pure fucking fatigue."

MORE CASTING STORIES

T O HEAR STORIES OF WHICH ACTORS AUDITioned for which alternate roles is to be thrust into a surreal alternate universe. Imagine, for instance, Tony Sirico as Uncle Junior or Big Pussy, both roles he read for before becoming Paulie Walnuts. Or Frank Vincent as Junior instead of Phil Leotardo; Van Zandt as Tony Soprano instead of Silvio; John Ventimiglia as practically every role other than Artie Bucco, including Christopher and Paulie. "I had a few friends who decided not to come in to the audition. I considered blowing it off myself," Ventimiglia says. "Who knew it was going to be a masterpiece?"

Most famously, Lorraine Bracco first read the part of Carmela, a part much closer to the *Goodfellas* role that had made her famous. "I told David that I had already done that. I'd always played the wife. It wasn't that interesting to me," Bracco says. "But as we were ending our conversation, I said, 'I have to tell you, I love this Jennifer Melfi character.'"

Climbing the stairs to the audition space, Jamie-Lynn Sigler and Robert Iler could hardly have expected they were about to begin an adolescence that would be observed in millions of American households. Sigler had worked strictly in musical theater. "I was at that age when I was too old to play a little girl but too young for most other roles. So, when I heard that I'd been sent on an audition for something called *The Sopranos*, I was thrilled. I assumed it had to do with music." After her audition, the producers told her they were interested but were worried she might be a little too tan. "I spent the week before the screen test loofah-ing like crazy, never going near a window and wearing long sleeves," Sigler says. "And it was the dead of August." (Iler, meanwhile, had an easier time of it. "All I did was come in and say the line, 'What? No fuckin' ziti then?' about twenty times," he says.)

At times, Chase has played a hunch when it comes to casting—none so bizarre or ultimately rewarding as the case of Steven Van Zandt. The man who would become Silvio Dante had, of course, already enjoyed a storied music career, both as a member of Bruce Springsteen's E Street Band and a solo artist. For the several years leading up to *The Sopranos*, however, he had dropped out of the music business—or, for that matter, any other business. "I spent seven years literally just walking my dog," Van Zandt says. "I didn't work at all. I was just sort of meditating and reflecting on my crazy world. I wasn't depressed really, just reflecting. It was a strange moment."

Chase had been a longtime fan of Springsteen and first noticed Van Zandt's photo on various E Street Band album covers; his stroke of genius was to see past Van Zandt's trademark head-scarves to the face beneath. "He looked like a Jersey Italian," Chase says, "which he is." Still, it took a remarkable series of accidents and near-misses to get Van Zandt cast: The singer had been drafted to induct the classic Jersey band *The Rascals* into the Rock and Roll Hall of Fame. It was the first time the induction ceremony had been televised and Chase just happened to catch Van Zandt's speech while flipping through channels. He resolved to track the musician down.

"I didn't have an agent or anything. There was no way to contact me," Van Zandt says. "Luckily, [casting director]

TOP ROW: Casting photos of Tony Sirico (Paulie Walnuts), Vincent Pastore ("Big Pussy" Bonpensiero), Lorraine Bracco (Dr. Jennifer Melfi), and Nancy Marchand (Livia Soprano). MIDDLE ROW: Edie Falco (Carmela Soprano), Robert Iler (A.J. Soprano), and John Ventimiglia (Artie Bucco). BOTTOM ROW: Dominic Chianese (Corrado "Junior" Soprano), Jamie-Lynn Sigler (Meadow Soprano), Michael Imperioli (Christopher Moltisanti), and Drea de Matteo (Adriana La Cerva).

TONY SIRICO

Edie Falco

bert Iler

Jamie-Lynn Sigler

Georgianne Walken is like Sherlock Holmes." Even then, it took a lot of convincing before Van Zandt agreed to consider a role. "I wasn't an actor. And even if I *was* I didn't want to be doing *television*," he says. "Television wasn't cool then like it is since *The Sopranos*." Years before, Van Zandt had invented a character named Silvio Dante. Reluctant to take a day-player's job, he suggested resurrecting the character. David then wrote it into the plot, and the rest is well-coiffed history.

Chase has always shown a willingness to reward good actors with expanded roles. Joe Gannascoli's Vito Spatafore began life on *The Sopranos* as an extra waiting in line in a bakery, eventually being used more and more until, at his own suggestion, an entire storyline about his character's homosexuality was born. (Gannascoli had always exhibited ambition before; when Ralph Cifaretto was killed, the actor called Landress to remind her that he would now be a Soprano Family captain. "Maybe in real life," Landress told him, "but I'm not sure it works that way on the show.")

But the most successful day-player of all was Drea de Matteo, who appeared in the pilot as an unnamed restaurant hostess and rose to the rank of mob princess. De Matteo had read for the part of Irina, Tony's Russian *goomara*, but was told that she was too WASPy to play any other roles on the show. "They said they could see me as this snooty, Connecticut-type hostess turning down Lorraine Bracco, so I said, 'Sure, I'll do it. Lorraine Bracco's awesome!' I was so nervous that it took me like fifteen takes to say my one line."

Nevertheless, a year later, de Matteo got a call for another small role, this time as Christopher's date. The scene was outside of a nightclub (an ersatz Martin Scorsese is seen entering in a storm of flashbulbs); one of the character's only lines was "Ow," when Christopher pulls her arm. "This time, before I went in, I was

going to make myself super Italian. I was at my grandmother's house in Queens, eating a chicken parmesan sandwich. I dug up this diamond nameplate necklace and made my hair as big as I could. I was going to be the only fucking guinea in that place," de Matteo says. "When my mother dropped me off at Silvercup, she said, 'Make sure you say the line like a girl from Queens. Make it like eighteen syllables.' So that's how I did it:

'Owwuhwwuhwwwuhwwwuh!' And that's how I got the part."

"IT WAS MAYHAM!"
—PAULIE WALNUTS

BY OCTOBER 1997, *THE SOPRANOS* PILOT HAD been shot and completed, a fact that seems to have meant near nothing for the show's prospects of ever making it onto the air. "It's really like a lottery, the tiny percentage of pilots that get picked up," says Edie Falco. "We had fun shooting the pilot, and at the end David said, 'You guys are great. Unfortunately no one is ever going to see this thing.' I was mostly excited to get paid something like $50,000 so I could clear some credit card debt."

Screening the pilot for the cast and friends had convinced Chase that he had something good. But, well-seasoned by previous failures, he equally was prepared for HBO to pull the plug. In fact, he had already developed what he calls "the beauty part of my plan": He planned to beg HBO for another $750,000 to shoot another forty-five minutes and release the product as a feature film. "Then I was off to Cannes," he says, laughing. "I mean, I didn't really want to do another TV series." Unfortunately for him (and for Cannes) the call came just before Christmas: HBO wanted twelve more episodes.

When *The Sopranos* debuted in January 1999, critical acclaim was swift. "It was an avalanche of praise," recalls Grey. "I had never seen such a unanimous response by such esteemed writers and critics. I think we were all stunned." Tony Soprano, one critic wrote, is a "marvel of baffled machismo." "*The Sopranos* may be the apotheosis of television drama," another chimed in. "Nearly everything about the show is brilliant." A writer for the *Sacramento Bee* seemed to sum up the consensus in a welter of adjectives: "It recalibrated the scale for comparing TV shows. Everything else seems flawed compared to this smart, nuanced, deep, rich, funny, touching, blunt, your-praise-here series."

More amazingly—since critical success by no means automatically translates to popularity—the audience seemed to love the show. Monday mornings were suddenly reserved for discussing the show in offices. The largely unknown cast members were surprised

Appearances in *Rolling Stone* (previous spread), *TV Guide* (above), and *MAD* magazine (opposite) confirmed the arrival of a new cultural juggernaut.

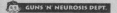

to find themselves recognized on the street. Every possible manifestation of pop cultural success followed: *MAD* magazine parodies and appearances on *The Simpsons*; video and pinball games; the cover of *Rolling Stone* and *TV Guide* and academic conferences with such presentations as "Coming Heavy: Intertextuality and Genre in *The Sopranos*"; and, of course, awards: at last count, eighteen Emmys®, including the first ever Best Dramatic Series to be won by a cable show, five Golden Globes, two Peabodys, and two Writers Guild Awards, among many others. "It's something of a miracle," says Grey. "I mean, a critical success and a commercial success that happens to have become my favorite TV show of all time? Can you imagine something like that in Hollywood?"

In the years since its debut, the show itself has grown in almost every quantifiable way. Episodes that once took eight days to film now take as many as fifteen. The binders filled with each episode's costume continuity photos have expanded from slim to jumbo. The number of actors considered "series regulars" has shot up from ten to twenty-six. In part such growth has been the necessary effect of the ever-expanding storyline. "More characters mean more costumes, more sets, more shooting days, more everything," says executive pro-

ducer Henry Bronchtein. Plus, as Landress points out, there are the peculiarities of mob life. "Every time you write in a new mobster, you need to give them a hangout and you have to hire four or five people to be their crew," she says. "You can't have a mobster without their crew." The result has been a ten-year cultural juggernaut.

Given all this, has David Chase revised his view of television? The answer seems to be extremely qualified. "I can't argue with destiny," he says, though he hastens to add, "I still feel as though film has more potential than TV. You're there in the dark. It overwhelms you. And it's a group experience, rather than an isolating experience, which TV is."

That said, of all the signs of *The Sopranos*'s success, Chase says that his proudest moments have been when New York's Museum of Modern Art announced it would acquire the show's first two seasons as part of its permanent collection (the only TV drama ever so chosen) and when he learned that people were getting together Sunday nights for "*Sopranos* parties."

"I loved that it was becoming communal," he says. "That meant everything to me. Who wouldn't want to be responsible for people having parties?"

CHASE'S MOB INFLUENCES

DAVID CHASE'S FIRST MEMORIES OF A MOB MOVIE are as a ten-year-old repeatedly watching the classic James Cagney movie *The Public Enemy* on the "Million Dollar Movie." (In those pre-cable days, a local station in New York showed the same movies five times a week.) In Willam Wellman's movie, mobster Tommy Powers (Cagney) rises through the ranks during Prohibition, becoming more and more ruthless and feuding both with rival gangs and his sanctimonious younger brother, a WWI veteran. In the end, he reconciles with his family only to be kidnapped by a rival gang and delivered home gruesomely wrapped like a mummy. "The END of Tom Powers is the end of every hoodlum," read the somber end titles, "*The Public Enemy* is not a man, nor is it a character—it is a problem that sooner or later WE, the public, must solve."

Chase was entranced, and not just by the gunplay. "The clothes and the cars looked like pictures I'd seen

of my father when he was young. I had an Uncle Tommy, who was the black sheep of the family. And in some ways, the Irish mother reminded me of my grandmother—soft and sweet, a nice immigrant woman. I felt like I was looking at my roots."

Though set in the world of the Irish mob during Prohibition, *The Public Enemy* also contained many of the darker elements that would later define the mob genre, including *The Sopranos*: glamour and violence; a complicated family (distant father, cluelessly doting mother, judgmental brother); the hypocrisy of the straight world; an attempt at redemption; and a bloody end. "It frightened me to death," Chase says. "I'd never seen machine guns and violence like that. When Cagney is delivered home at the end, I was scared shitless."

Scenes from *The Public Enemy* (this page) and *The Godfather: Part I* (opposite).

Of course, the more modern and direct influences on *The Sopranos* are the movies of Martin Scorsese: *Mean Streets, Goodfellas,* and most notably *Raging Bull,* and also Francis Ford Coppola's *The Godfather* trilogy. *The Sopranos* began life with its mob movie pedigree intact, featuring, as it did, Dominic Chianese, who had appeared in *The Godfather: Part II,* Lorraine Bracco, who had played Mrs. Henry Hill, and Michael Imperioli, who had a small but unforgettable part in Scorsese's movie as Spider, who is shot in the foot (and later elsewhere) by Joe Pesci's Tommy DeVito.

Still, the nascent TV hit was careful not to overdo it. "We didn't want to look too much like any other movie," says executive producer Ilene Landress. "We loved Frank Vincent as an actor early on. But he had been so memorable as Billy Batts in *Goodfellas* that we couldn't do it. Then, as we became established, we could say, 'Hey he's great. Go get him.'"

Chase happily admits that he "idolizes and lionizes" Scorsese's work, but he points out that a major difference between it and *The Sopranos* is that the television show takes place in the present—which means that the characters may themselves have watched *Goodfellas* and, in some cases, styled themselves based on the movie. Certainly, that's the case with *The Godfather* movies—or simply I, II, III, no further explanation needed. For the Soprano crew, the trilogy is the urtext on what it

IT'S OFTEN BEEN SAID THAT MAFIA SOLDIERS NEVER RITUALLY KISSED EACH OTHER UNTIL *THE GODFATHER* TAUGHT THEM HOW.

means to be a mobster—even when they're badly mangling their quotes: ("Louis Brasi sleeps with the fishes," says Christopher. "*Luca Brazzi,*" Big Pussy scolds him.)

In some ways, *The Godfather* is the source of dangerous illusions. When Tony bemoans the loss of honor and duty in The Family, he's speaking as much about the fictional world of Mario Puzo and Francis Ford Coppola than anything that really existed. (It's often been said that Mafia soldiers never ritually kissed each other until *The Godfather* taught them how.) It's no accident that when Tony has an anxiety dream about fulfilling his role as boss he finds himself dressed like Michael Corleone, searching in vain for a gun taped behind a toilet. His life is no sepia-toned epic.

Chase and company have never been shy about tipping their hats to these and other influences. After Livia Soprano's funeral,

Tony comes home to find *The Public Enemy* on TV. Watching Cagney's doting mother, he begins to cry. When Uncle Junior dismisses his longtime *goomara,* he shoves a cake in her face, a tribute to Cagney's famous use of a grapefruit to dump his girlfriend. Silvio Dante, of course, is famous within the crew for his impressions of Al Pacino as Corleone.

Other references may be more the work of overactive fan minds. When the attempt is made on Tony's life at the end of Season One, he's carrying a carton of orange juice. A reference to Don Corleone buying oranges before he was shot? Perhaps. When Phil Leotardo kills Angelo Garepe in the trunk of his car, was it some sort of karmic payback for Billy Batts's similar fate in *Goodfellas*? You decide. As Christopher says when he shoots a bakery counterman in the foot—a strangely familiar scene: "It happens."

CHAPTER 2

WELCOME TO

NEW JERSEY

A SENSE OF PLACE

JERSEY.

YOU CAN FORGET THE "NEW."

IT'S NOT NECESSARY. NOBODY WOULD EVER SAY "YORK" OR "HAMPSHIRE" IN REFERRING TO THOSE OTHER "NEW" STATES. BUT SAY "JERSEY," AND YOU KNOW EXACTLY WHERE YOU ARE—

maybe even more accurately than when you use the more formal, two-word version. While "New Jersey" is a perfectly nice legal entity with a letterhead and an official seal and a Department of Education and such, "Jersey" is something else altogether—a set of values and traditions and neuroses and, possibly, hairstyles. New Jersey may be a state, but Jersey is a state of mind.

THE SOPRANOS TAKES PLACE IN JERSEY.

IT'S OFTEN BEEN SAID THAT THE GARDEN State functions as a *Sopranos* character in its own right, its suburbo-industrial landscapes—from railroad bridges to cineplexes, working-class row houses to McMansions—as vital to the feel of the show as gunplay, familial angst, or trays of ziti.

This sense of place was an integral part of David Chase's vision for the show. "I always wanted to shoot the Meadowlands," he says of the spooky, swampy wetlands that form a backdrop to so much of *The Sopranos* action, particularly in its early seasons. "Even when I was a child, my parents used to drive me through here and I'd think, *What is this place? This is amazing.*"

Though born in Mt. Vernon, New York, Chase grew up in North Caldwell, New Jersey—the same suburb in which Tony and Carmela live. Coming home was crucial when it came to finding the characters that would inhabit *The Sopranos*. "I've always had trouble writing characters unless I can picture them in places I know from my childhood," Chase says, recalling the TV movie he wrote in 1980 called *Off the Minnesota Strip*. "It was about a teenage prostitute who goes back to her small town in Minnesota. We went out to the Midwest, but I just couldn't get it. I couldn't write the fucking thing until I pictured this girl in Caldwell."

THIS SENSE OF PLACE WAS AN INTEGRAL PART OF DAVID CHASE'S VISION.

"There's so much of everything in New Jersey," says director of photography Phil Abraham. "You have factories and freeways and the Meadowlands and strip malls. They all kind of commingle."

Like thousands of others, Chase's Italian family had started their American journey in the section of Newark then known as the First Ward. In the early part of the 20th century, the First Ward—also known as the North Ward or Seventh Avenue—was said to be the fifth largest Italian population outside of Italy. It was, by all accounts, a sepia-toned, nostalgist's dream of the Old Neighborhood—a teeming enclave of bakeries and fruit stalls, hard-working craftsmen, and sharp-dressed gangsters. The community was centered around St. Lucy's church, famous for its annual Feast of St. Gerard during which a statue of the saint was paraded down the street adorned with dollar bills. (A version of the ongoing festival, renamed the Feast of St. Elzear, figured prominently in *The Sopranos*'s Season Six episode "The Ride." "We had tried to do some kind of feast show for eight years," says Chase.)

Vibrant as it was, the First Ward was no match for the so-called "urban renewal" initiatives of the 1950s, which replaced large swaths of the neighborhood with housing projects. A series of race riots in 1967 completed the transformation as the remaining white population took flight. By the 1970s, the most Italian thing about Seventh Avenue was the name of the Christopher Columbus housing projects.

The fact is that the First Ward's Italian population would likely have moved on with or without such sociopolitical pressures. Such is the story of immigration in America—and in New Jersey in particular. The dream is to always be moving toward the next bigger house, the next town up the road. The route for First Warders was clear: if you didn't head across the river to New York, you moved west along Bloomfield Avenue. That street provides both a literal and figurative spine to the geography of *The Sopranos*. It runs from the First Ward, through such working-class neighborhoods as West Orange (where Livia lives), into Montclair (home to Dr. Melfi's office), and finally to upscale suburbs like Hanover and Roseland, the Oranges, and the Caldwells. "That was the journey for the wise guys," says Chase.

Above: Livia Soprano's house. Right: "One of the things I loved about this show is that it made older people powerful," says James Gandolfini. "They're tough, funny, vindictive people. Uncle Junior still likes women, still likes to fuck. He's not on *Golden Girls*."

THE JERSEY LOOK

ALL OF NEW JERSEY'S MOVING and striving, dreaming and resenting, has left its mark on the physical landscape. As befits the most densely settled state in America, the Jersey "look" may best be defined as a kind of hypereclecticism, with all manner of building and vista piled on top of each other.

"There's so much of everything in New Jersey," says director of photography Phil Abraham. "You have factories and freeways and the Meadowlands and strip malls. They all kind of commingle."

"Nothing is ever done in one style," says production designer Bob Shaw, whose eye for detail may be most responsible for the verisimilitude of *The Sopranos* look. Shaw joined the show after its first season. In the years since he has attended hundreds of location scouts and spent countless hours poking through houses up and down the Garden State Parkway. He is probably about as much an authority on New Jersey style as any man alive.

In part, the state's eclecticism can be chalked up to a constant state of change: As one population after another made their way, either literally or metaphorically, up Bloomfield Avenue, each left its mark on the landscape. "When these towns changed, it wasn't always a smooth transition," says Shaw, who himself grew up in Mountain Lakes, New Jersey. "A family would move out of a large house in Jersey City and someone else would come and chop it in half, or thirds, or quarters. In order to comply with some city code, maybe they put a fire escape on what had been a Dutch Colonial house. Or they saw a deluxe, beveled-glass door with side lights at Home Depot and thought it would be perfect. All these things stacked up over the years."

What Shaw sees in the living rooms of New Jerseyites—and, by extension, what we see in *The Sopranos* homes, from Carmela's Roman-column TV pedestal to Christopher's "Master-of-the-Universe" leather-and-steel furniture set—could be called the aesthetic of aspiration. And it, too, creates a wildly diverse look.

"It's like people have a checklist of what signifies luxury: a curved staircase and a landing and a great room that's two stories tall and a Jacuzzi and two sinks," says Shaw. "The problem is that all these things don't necessarily go together. Lately, it's turrets. You'll see a fairly conventional house with a turret in the middle of it. It's like a merit badge they need for their house: the Turret Badge."

Carmela's taste in clothes, as well as in the way she decorates her house, can be called "the aesthetic of aspiration," and can be seen throughout homes in New Jersey.

THE OPENING CREDITS

HISTORIANS TELL US THAT THE LINCOLN Tunnel, connecting Weehawken, New Jersey, with midtown Manhattan, was completed and opened to traffic in December 1937. Logically, this would mean that, at some point, it was possible to emerge from the tiled tunnel and pull up at the New Jersey Turnpike tollbooth without having a soundtrack of "Woke Up This Morning" in one's head. Frankly, this is hard to imagine. "The idea

was just to have Tony leaving New York and driving home," says David Chase of his show's opening credits.

Director of photography Phil Abraham and director Allen Coulter shot the sequence over a day and a half with a 16mm camera. (You can see Abraham's light-tan colored pants reflected in the windshield as Tony pulls up to the tollbooth.) "It was very documentary style," he says. "I was just pointing the camera at what looked interesting and shooting it."

Still, in just over a minute and a half, the credits tell a densely packed story. Tony's journey—out of New York, through the industrial swamps of the Meadowlands and working-class neigh-

borhoods of Newark and finally into the high-end suburbs—tells all you need to know about the show's fictional world and has deeper resonance than a simple drive home.

Of all the locations captured in the sequence, only Satriale's Pork Store is a fake; the set was built in an abandoned auto parts store store in Kearny, New Jersey, and maintained for the life of the series. (The store's inclusion is a remnant of an earlier credits concept in which Tony would pass various other of *The Sopranos* characters on his drive.) In six seasons, the sequence was changed only

As for the music, Chase and producer Martin Bruestle tried the edited footage alongside several different songs, including tracks by The Kinks, Little Stevie, and a band called Funky Green Dogs. Luckily, Chase remembered a song he'd heard on Los Angeles public radio by an obscure English band called Alabama 3 (later shortened, for legal reasons, to A3 in the U.S.).

"From that point on, it was history," Bruestle says. "It was the perfect example of playing a piece of music against a piece of film and both of them are somehow elevated by their marriage."

ON LOCATION IN JERSEY

ALTHOUGH A HANDFUL OF RECURRING SETS— Dr. Melfi's office, the Soprano house, Nuovo Vesuvio restaurant—are built at Silvercup Studios in Queens, the distinctive look of *The Sopranos* has always rested on Chase's determination to shoot on location as much as possible. If it takes ten to twelve days to shoot an episode, an average of eight will be spent in New Jersey. Where exactly is the responsibility of the locations department.

visiting rooms and Irish-American associations (like the one next to Satriale's) into Italian social clubs. (Occasionally, the production does cross state lines for one reason or another: New York's Harriman State Park became the Jersey Pine Barrens for the episode in which Christopher and Paulie get lost in the woods. Some scenes on Tony's boat, *The Stugots*, are shot on Staten Island.)

When scouts return from the field, they meticulously paste their photos into manila folders. By the middle of Season Six, the locations office had an estimated 14,000 folders stored in dozens of filing cabinets. The cabinets have labels like BILLIARD HALLS, BINGO HALLS, BODY DUMP SITES. This is the kind of place where conversations begin, "We're looking for a place to throw a head down a sewage drain . . ." and nobody even blinks.

(Above) The Soprano house is in Caldwell, New Jersey. (Opposite) Vito Spatafore's New Hampshire scenes were shot in Boonton, New Jersey.

At any given time, in all seasons and all weather, there are at least four location scouts pounding the pavement across northern Jersey, ringing doorbells and taking panoramic photos of every conceivable type of building from every conceivable angle. If you happen to be looking for an electrical plant or a Laundromat or a nail salon or a casino or a house where you can see a cemetery out the window or an abandoned clearing where two drivers can pull up next to each other and have a serious conversation . . . well, the locations office probably has ten of each.

Over the years, the scouts have found corners of New Jersey that look like a college in Maine (scenes of Tony and Meadow visiting colleges were shot at Drew University in Madison) and a bucolic New Hampshire hamlet (Vito Spatafore actually fled to Boonton). They've turned public-school gymnasiums into prison

Whether a building looks right for a scene is only the first of many questions that location managers Gina Heyman and April Taylor need to answer. (The two alternate episodes, one prepping the next script while the other films.) Will the owners agree? How much money will they want? Is there enough parking for sixty crew cars and fifteen trailers, six of them eighteen-wheelers? Space for 125 crew members, plus actors and extras who in, say, a scene at the Bada Bing, might number another seventy-five bartenders, strippers, and customers? Will the local town government divert traffic? Are there enough bathrooms? Electrical hookups? Places for catering? And so on. "We have eight days to get it all together," says Heyman. "And basically we're in a panic the whole time."

Still, it's an item of faith on the show that all this effort is worth it to get New Jersey—the real New Jersey—on the screen in all its tacky/classy, goofy/serious, ugly/beautiful splendor. "We even shoot interiors in New Jersey. David believes that somehow you can tell the difference," says Heyman. "And he's probably right."

Ext. Small Town (Boonton NJ)

Main St. btw. Planes 𝕝 & School 𝕝

TONY AND CARMELA'S LUXURIOUS

NORTH JERSEY

McMANSION

THE SOPRANO HOUSE,

in all its sprawling glory, resides intact on one stage—Stage "X"—at Silvercup Studios. Aside from the fact that the ceilings are a lighting grid and many walls can be wheeled aside for easier filming, the set maintains the geography of a real Jersey McMansion.

THE FAMILY ROOM

The books that set decorator Janet Shaw assembled for Season One (mostly pulp novels, including Mario Puzo, sports, and history books) have gone largely untouched. "This is not a house where you sit around at night reading novels," Shaw says.

CARMELA'S KITCHEN

The kitchen underwent a renovation before Season Six, complete with new countertops, appliances, and window treatments. Says Janet Shaw, "Carmela's one of those people who just buys everything at once. When we first built the set, everything had to match: the curtains, the placemats, the towels, right down to the oven mitts."

THE DINING ROOM

Few rooms in the Soprano house are as important as the dining room, site of Sunday family dinner. The dining room table expands to accomodate the favored few chosen to dine with the Boss—and contracts to shut out those who have lost their seat.

THE BEDROOMS

The Soprano house is littered with signifiers of what it means to be rich and successful, from the bidet in Tony and Carmela's bathroom to the mock Renaissance painting above their dresser *(left)*. Meadow's room *(top right)* still shows signs of being a little princess's domain, while A.J.'s *(bottom right)* testifies to his lack of discipline.

CURL UP AND

HAIR AND MAKEUP IN NEW JERSEY

"SOMETIMES I'M IN THE GROCERY STORE AND I just stare," says Kymbra Callaghan, who shares makeup duty with her husband, Steve Kelley, and herself lives in New Jersey. "People think you're crazy, but you can't help it."

"They wear an insane amount of makeup," says Kelley. "Everything is done up to the point where, if we reproduced it on film, people would say we've gone too far."

For most characters, though, a more subtle approach is in order. Carmela's hair is slightly teased and her use of makeup is what you might call liberal, but she remains within the bounds of fashion. "You want her to be attractive, but still just a little bit Jersey," says hairstylist Anthony Veader.

Meadow Soprano avoided the worst of the Jersey treatment while in high school. "David wanted her to be Daddy's little girl. For a long time,

"The Vixen"

"The Housewife"

"The Jersey Updo"

"The Sophisticate"

DYE:

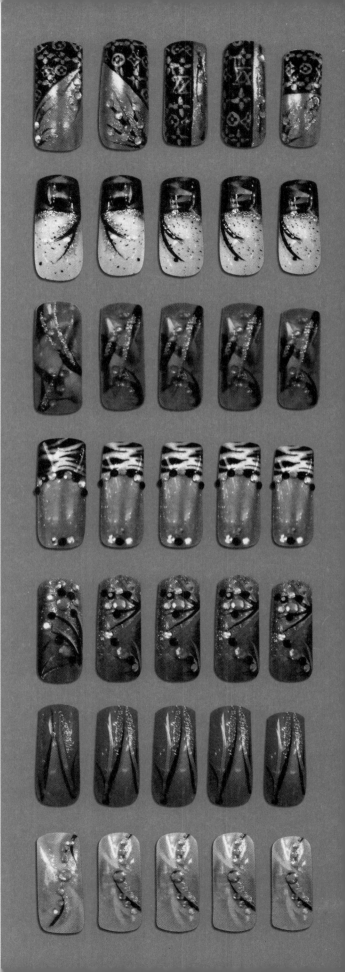

her makeup was very simple to keep her that way," Callaghan says. Meadow later returned from Columbia University with a pointedly more sophisticated sense of style. Janice Soprano, meanwhile, solidified her shift from Seattle hippie to putative Mafia wife in part through the sudden application of hairspray and foundation.

But while the stylists discuss such looks with dutiful interest and a sense of satisfaction, there's no hiding the joy with which they turn to *The Sopranos*'s other great female character: Adriana La Cerva. "Oh it was great doing Adriana," says Callaghan. "She was a real Jersey girl."

Nothing said 'Adriana La Cerva' like a set of elaborate nails. Over the years, *The Sopranos*'s makeup department—with the help of a stylist named Maria Salandra at Finger Fitness Nail Salon in Cliffside Park, N.J.—truly pushed the bounds of digital fashion. "Basically we tried every pattern you can think of," says Steve Kelley. "Leopard spots, tiger and zebra stripes, jewels, Louis Vuitton logos, a nail to match virtually every one of her outfits. Nothing was too much for Adriana."

"SLEEPS WITH THE FISHES OUT OF WATER":

THE SOPRANOS AWAY

WHATEVER YOU'RE LOOKING FOR, YOU CAN find it in New Jersey," says location manager Regina Heyman. Perhaps, but even the location-rich Garden State has trouble coming up with sites that simulate Rodeo Drive, the Champs-Elysées, or the Cave of the Sybil. Occasionally, the Jersey gang (and *The Sopranos* crew) have had to pack up and take their show on the road.

In Season Six, Christopher headed west to Hollywood to pitch his film *Cleaver*, a trip most memorable for ending with Lauren Bacall being mugged for a gift basket. Later that same season, Carmela and Rosalie Aprile went to Paris. Carmela was wowed by the tides of history absent from even the oldest neighborhoods of Essex County. "We worry so much. Sometimes it seems that's all we do. But in the end, it all gets washed away," she said, in her moment of revelation.

Or appeared to say. In fact, Edie Falco had a terrible case of the flu during the entire shoot, which left her voice barely audible. If you notice Sharon Angela, who plays Rosalie, straining to hear in her scenes outside the Cluny Museum, it was because Falco had entirely lost her voice; all her dialogue was looped in later.

"I'd always complained about how the guys get to go to Italy and I'm stuck in the kitchen. Now, this was my big trip abroad and I was deathly sick," says Falco. "After every shot, everybody else would go out shopping and I'd sit in the bathtub and shiver."

The crew also got a lesson in the Continental style of filming. Production manager Mark Kamine says that the contract with the French crew required that red wine be served with lunch. "We were shooting at night, so sometimes 'lunch' was eight in the morning," Kamine says, not unadmiringly. "Sure enough, out would come the wine."

THE ITALIAN JOB

BUT NO *SOPRANOS* FIELD TRIP WAS AS memorable—for both the fictional characters and their creators—than when Tony, Paulie, and Christopher headed to Naples for the Season Two episode "Commendatori." The three were in the old country to negotiate a deal involving stolen cars. Christopher quickly hooked up with a fellow junkie and spent the trip nodding off in his hotel room. Tony passed the time with Annalisa, the voluptuous woman running the Neapolitan mob while her husband was in prison. In between fantasies of screwing Annalisa while wearing Roman centurion's garb, Tony managed to negotiate a deal that brought one of her soldiers, Furio Giunta, to north Jersey. Meanwhile, Paulie had a harrowing time confronting the gulf between Italian and Italian-American. Puzzled by Neapolitan cuisine, he asked for macaroni and gravy and was amazed when his prostitute wasn't more excited that their ancestors were from the same town. (It was just down the road and presumably she knew a lot of people from there.) "And you thought

Tony spends time with Annalisa, the head of the Neapolitan mob, during his crew's trip to Italy.

Germans were classless pieces of shit," one of Paulie's Italian companions told another.

As it happens, the real-life filming trip to Naples was scarcely less eventful. "We ate at a different restaurant every night. It was fantastic," says Tony Sirico who, like his character, was in the motherland for the first time. One night the actors visited a place that served *linguine con vongole*, linguine with clams, a Neapolitan specialty.

"Jim [Gandolfini] asked for grated cheese, but in Naples they don't put cheese on seafood pasta," remembers Michael Imperioli. "The waiter was very nice about it but he said, 'No.' I think we all thought it was a suggestion, but this wasn't open to discussion. 'No cheese.' That's how they do it over there."

Culinary confusion wasn't the only echo of the show they encountered: Somewhere along the line, the group had acquired a guide—a tough local kid named Max. On their last day in town, David Chase, Gandolfini, director Tim Van Patten, and Federico Castelluccio, who played Furio, arranged with Max to visit a teeming market outside the usual tourist sphere.

"It was a really tough spot," says Van Patten, getting into his story. "I mean like, guys with patches on their eyes and scars and stuff. At some point this guy comes barreling down the street and bumps into David and disappears." A few minutes later, Chase reached for his wallet and found it missing. He'd been pickpocketed.

"Max stands up in the middle of this crowded street and he says *'Attencione! Attencione!'* Nobody pays any attention. So, he says, 'My uncle is Signore so-and-so.' And, all of a sudden, everybody goes silent. Everybody stops. Max holds up his cell phone and says, 'If this man's wallet is not returned, I will dial my uncle.'"

Moments later, says Van Patten, a man quietly approached Max, whispered to him, and the two took off down the street with the Americans huffing and puffing behind. After a few blocks, Max stopped and pointed to a large man standing in a doorway. Sure enough, it was the man who had bumped into Chase.

"Now we're all jacked up. We surround him. Federico and I are on one side, David and Jim on the other. And Max walks up to this guy—much bigger than any of us. He points to David and says, 'Do you have this man's wallet?' And then he just hauls off and cracks this huge guy in the face. Boom! He says, 'If these people weren't here, I'd kill you.'"

As the Americans gaped, the thief straightened up and pointed to the gutter in front of him. There, under a car, was Chase's wallet, the money still inside.

"After that, Max was our hero. We were throwing money at him, we can't do enough for him," says Van Patten. "Four months later, we were back in New York. It was the dead of winter and we were shooting out on the street somewhere and, all of a sudden, we saw this familiar figure coming down the street." It was Max. "Where's David?" he asked. As it turned out, Max stayed in the States for two months, even living with Castelluccio for part of the time.

"After a while we had to think, *God was it all a set-up?*" Van Patten says. "I mean, it was just so perfect. Absolute genius. I guess we'll never know."

SEASON 6   EPISODE 11   TITLE   COLD STONE

"What's the matter with you? Why would you bring New Jersey here?"

ATTRIBUTION   —ROSALIE APRILE

CHAPTER 3

"ONCE YOU'RE IN THIS
THERE'S NO

FAMILY,
GETTING OUT"

MEET THE SOPRANOS

WE ARE A FAMILY.

AGE THAT MEANS SOMETHING."

—TONY SOPRANO

Which is more dangerous to a mobster's mental and physical health, his family or his Family? That's one of the jokes—not always so funny—on which *The Sopranos* is founded. After six seasons, the answer still isn't entirely clear.

Strip away all the specific mob trappings from *The Sopranos* and, in many ways, you're left with a classic American family story. The Soprano family itself, when we first met them, could have walked out of a 1950s suburban family sitcom: Hardworking dad, stay-at-home mom, two cute, mischievous kids, cranky, colorful old folks prone to irreverent comments. It was practically *Leave It to Beaver* with Jersey accents.

AS THE SHOW HAS GROWN, SO, BY NECESsity, has the family tree. Tony's older sister, Janice, of course, reentered the scene, and we've caught glimpses of his younger sister, Barbara, too, though she's relocated to upstate New York. We've met Carmela's family, the De Angelis clan, and Tony's cousins, the Blundettos, whose matriarch was Livia Soprano's sister. At times, the tree has required pruning and shaping: Christopher Moltisanti was connected to Tony principally through marriage; Carmela's father's sister, her aunt Lena, was Dickie Moltisanti's mother and Christopher's grandmother. Later, as the notion of family became more and more important to Tony, a tenuous connection to the Soprano side of the family was emphasized. It emerged that Dickie married a Blundetto, thus sealing his connection to Tony in blood.

Through this ever-expanding network, *The Sopranos* has explored universal familial themes: What does it mean to be a good father or mother? How do you deal with aging parents? Where is the balance between personal happiness and family well-being? How the hell are you supposed to get along with these people to whom you're both cursed and blessed to be related."

> ## "GROWING UP SOPRANO IS JUST PLAIN WEIRD."
> —A.J. SOPRANO

S TILL, IT WAS LEO TOLSTOY WHO WISELY wrote, "All happy families resemble one another, each unhappy family is unhappy in its own way." (The quote provided the title of the Season Five episode, "All Happy Families..."). For all the universality of their condition, the Sopranos and their associates certainly have family issues that are, well, unique. Fathers across the world may feel conflicted emotions about their sons possibly joining the family business; most don't have to worry that it will get the kid killed. Likewise, plenty of kids feel their parents are being hypocrites when they tell them what to do; not all that many can point to their father doing business out of the back of a strip club, let alone murdering people. And, of course, the older generation rarely plots to have a member of the younger one killed.

Other characters have equally baroque family involvements. Janice took over the raising of Bobby Bacala's two children (and they had one of their own) but she more or less abandoned her son, Harpo,

"You accord this little old woman an almost mystical ability to wreak havoc," Dr. Melfi told Tony, and you needed only to watch the poor admitting administrator at Green Grove Retirement Community squirm under Livia's unblinking stare to get a sense of why that was the case—and why Tony might be in therapy for a very long time to come.

David Chase has made no secret of the fact that Livia was based in large part on his own mother, Norma. In what one suspects is a case of understatement, he often refers to Norma Chase as "a difficult woman," "quite a character," and "funny, though not intentionally."

DAVID CHASE HAS MADE NO SECRET OF THE FACT THAT LIVIA WAS BASED IN LARGE PART ON HIS OWN MOTHER, NORMA.

from a previous relationship. Paulie Walnuts was forced to grapple with the revelation that his beloved Nucci, who raised him, was in fact his aunt. Brotherhood is of vast importance to both Phil Leotardo and Patsy Parisi, both of whom lose siblings to the mob life.

> ## "I'M SURE HE'S TELLING HIS PSYCHIATRIST IT'S ALL HIS MOTHER'S FAULT."
> —LIVIA SOPRANO

A ND THEN THERE'S LIVIA.
Of all the fearsome characters who have passed across *The Sopranos* screen—from impulsive psychopaths to cold-blooded killers—the scariest of all may still be a frail, gray-haired old lady, the family matriarch. As played by Nancy Marchand, who passed away from lung cancer between Seasons Two and Three, Livia Soprano entered every room with a toxic mixture of guilt, manipulation, insecurity, paranoia, and hostility—the whole spectrum of dysfunction.

"Everybody found her difficult to deal with," Chase says. "A shrink once told me that it might have been that she was spoiled. She was the second girl from the last out of eleven kids. By that point, my grandmother might have been so exhausted that my mother was really raised by her teenage siblings, who weren't very good at it." Chase's cousin Joe—a man he called "Uncle Junior"—once told him that Norma was easily teased as a child. Chase says she grew up to be a thin-skinned and paranoid woman who nonetheless had a gift for insulting others. Among the choicer bits of Chase family repartee was when Norma told David that she'd rather see him dead than avoid the Vietnam War draft. (He had a back injury). When he called home to say he'd directed his first TV show—an episode of *Alfred Hitchcock Presents*—his mother expressed disbelief. "Really? Did they accept it?" she asked.

If growing up with Norma was complicated, at least it made writing for Livia Soprano easy. "'Poor you,' 'I don't answer the phone after dark,' 'Ooh, he's another one'—all of those lines were straight out of my mother's mouth," Chase says. But perhaps just as crucial to *The Sopranos* view of family was Chase's father, Henry. It had been Henry's mother who changed the family name from DeCesare to Chase. A Baptist, originally from Providence, Rhode Island, Henry was raised in a house run by a petty tyrant, Chase says. "His father was a prick. A really mean motherfucker," he says, adding that his maternal grandfather was much the same. "Both of these guys came over from the other side in the late 19th and early 20th centuries and they were tough, hard men, bad guys to deal with. In that world, women and children were supposed to be seen and not heard."

Henry had had a chance to go to medical school before the Great Depression forced him to work instead. When David

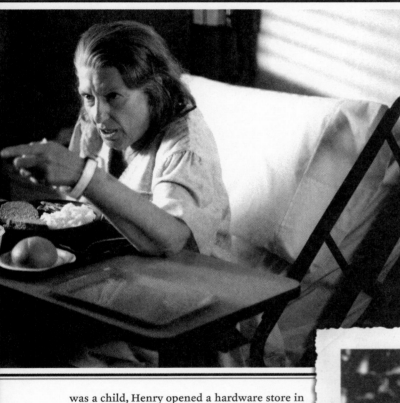

was a child, Henry opened a hardware store in Verona, New Jersey, at just about the time such small, personally owned businesses were beginning to be subsumed, crushed by larger chain stores. (Here may be the seeds of Paulie's eventual vendetta against corporate coffee shops.) "He was a disappointed man. An angry man," Chase says of his father. "It made him sullen and pissy around the house."

But beyond missed opportunities, a difficult wife, business problems, and whatever

other concerns he might have harbored, what ate away at the elder Chase was a condition Tony Soprano would recognize all too well: The gulf between what he believed family *should* be and what his own family actually was. "My father was very conscientious about being a good father, a good brother, a good son. And at the same time, his family was constantly riddled by factionalism and grudges, schisms, and feuds that went on for decades. His mother had taken up with another man and there was always fighting between the siblings," Chase says. "Maybe that's why he was so angry, because he really wanted the family to stick together."

Tony feels just such a conflicted sense of duty and the same keen frustration that things aren't as they should be. Livia might have insisted that "daughters are better at taking care of their mothers than sons" (an actual Norma Chase quote), but it was Janice and Barbara who fled the family while Tony stayed to perform the thankless task of looking after Livia. It's Tony who berates himself for being an ungrateful, bad son, even after he learns his mother tried to have him whacked; and it's Tony who fears, almost above all else, that he has passed on his sense of emptiness and depression to his own son and who beats himself

"I COULD STICK THIS FORK IN YOUR EYE!"

—LIVIA SOPRANO

Above and below: Livia, Johnny, and Junior Soprano in the 1960s.

up for not loving A.J. enough; who twists himself into knots sticking by scheming Janice and fucked-up Christopher and fading Uncle Junior; who still reflexively struggles to protect Livia's memory when she's dead: "She loved you very much," he tells Meadow, despite scant evidence that the old lady was capable of any such thing.

At such moments, when Tony weeps watching the idealized, adoring mobster mother in *The Public Enemy* or when a happy clan of ducks reminds him of everything he doesn't have, what we're seeing may be a little bit of Henry Chase's rage and confusion at how something as pure and good as family can turn out to be so messy, so painful, and so flawed.

IN LOVING
REMEMBRANCE OF

LIVIA
SOPRANO
1930–2001

Gone but not forgotten

A precious one from us has gone
A voice we loved is stilled;
A place is vacant in our home,
Which never can be filled.
God in His wisdom has recalled,
The boon his love had given,
And though the body slumbers here,
The soul is safe in Heaven.

A SHORT STORY ABOUT NANCY MARCHAND, TOLD BY JOHN VENTIMIGLIA

"I got to work with her once. It was the last episode of the first season and Livia was in the hospital. Artie Bucco was bringing her some food in her room. In fact, Livia wound up telling Artie that it was Tony who burned down Vesuvio's.

Anyway, between takes we had some downtime and Nancy was lying in bed. And she started reading aloud to me from a newspaper. She was reading the obituary of, like, a Czechoslovakian circus performer—all about the history of his acrobatic troupe and his life and how he became a performer. Then the article went into his particular skills, how he could walk on his hands and had mastered the trapeze. Finally, she had been reading for so long that I came around behind her to see the article for myself and it turned out to be just an advertising insert. Nancy looked at me and winked. She'd been making it all up off the top of her head for my benefit. It was just a wonderful, generous thing to do. It was a gift."

DOMINIC CHIANESE ON

"UNCLE JUNIOR" SOPRANO

"THERE'S A DESPERATE QUALITY ABOUT UNCLE JUNIOR: DESPER-ATE FOR POWER, FOR MONEY, FOR SECURITY, TO BE NEEDED. At one time he had a family. He had a girlfriend. He had a sister-in-law he loved very much. He had power. And all of it slipped away from him—until he wound up alone in an institution.

He's smart like a dog is smart. Watchful. Suspicious. He blames the world for making him feel powerless and weak. He blames his nephew, Tony. He blames Carmela for shutting the door in his face. He blames everybody but himself. Basically, he's an insecure person, and he uses humor to cover up his insecurities. Uncle Junior wouldn't be Uncle Junior if he wasn't funny.

His brother Johnny, Tony's father, was always more powerful than Junior. I think there was a little jealousy there, though he loves Tony tremendously. He sees himself play-ing baseball with him when he was a kid. Uncle Junior does have a heart. I think the idea of killing his nephew bothered him, drove him crazy. But his nephew was going to take his power away and the one thing he can't stand is being disrespected.

In part, he misses the old days. His neighborhood is changing. The world is changing. He misses the simplicity of the old habits—family dinners, meeting guys at the social club. The old ways. He might have tried to kill Tony but he would never snitch on him. Junior's loyalty to his cause is very strong. It's all he has.

He never got married because, first of all, he's too cheap. He didn't want a woman to spend all his money. He did keep Roberta as a 'friend' for sixteen years. He ended that because she talked about him performing certain acts on her. All the men probably did that, but you weren't supposed to talk about it. It made you look unmasculine. Like you didn't have any balls. But I think what bugged Junior is that she didn't keep it quiet. She was disloyal. That, to him, is a terrible thing.

There was a scene where Tony and Junior were sitting on the couch in his house and Tony asked Junior if he loved him. I think the question really hit home. There were all kinds of emotions involved: Shame. Guilt. Regret. And it was probably his first realization that he was suffering from memory loss. He wasn't sure who was asking the question. In any event, he was scared to answer. It was too personal.

Still, Junior is stubborn and he's tough. He'll kill you if he has to. An insecure man is a very dan-gerous thing."

JOY OF SPECS

FEW THINGS CAN EXPRESS the gulf between Uncle Junior Soprano and Dominic Chianese more succinctly than this: Chianese doesn't like to curse. "I've always had an aversion to the F-word," says the gentlemanly actor whose character is responsible for such bon mots as "Anthony is a cunt hair away from owning all of northern Jersey. I am that cunt hair," and "Federal marshals are so far up my ass I can taste Brylcreem."

Helping bridge the gap between Chianese, the demure actor, and Junior, the foul-mouthed don, are Uncle Junior's signature over-sized glasses. "They give me an actual mask to hide behind," says Chianese, whose acting credits include both Shakespeare and a role in *The Godfather: Part II*. "They actually change my eyesight. They make every-body's heads bigger. And if I look in the mirror, I see a different set of eyes looking back. I won't even do rehearsals without them. They *are* the character."

TONY SOPRAN

"TONY SOPRANO IS JUST A KID FROM JERSEY, STRUGGLING TO GET ALONG LIKE EVERYBODY ELSE. He makes mistakes like everybody else. It's just that his mistakes have more serious consequences.

Tony made a choice early on. He had tried another way—he had his semester and a half at college—but that's not how he was raised. He didn't exactly have the best home life. He probably wanted to impress his father. And working for a living is *hard*. So, he made his choice. Maybe it was the easy way out that ended up being the more difficult way out. Most easy ways out usually do.

When we first met Tony, it was starting to weigh on him. He was realizing that the way of life he'd devoted himself to wasn't what he thought it would be. He thought there would be a code and honor, but in the end it was just every man for himself. He thought, *I'm 40 years old. What the fuck am I doing? I'm killing myself and for what? I have the nice house, the nice car, the nice clothes and all of that, and I still have to deal with all this petty horseshit.* And of course he's got that Soprano gene: depression.

I don't think Tony had a burning desire to be the boss. Not like his uncle, who wanted it badly. He's just one of those people who thinks things should be done in a particular way and gets frustrated when it's not. Of course, his idea of solving a problem is to blow up his friend's restaurant because he can't stop a guy from getting killed there. That's his way of doing a good deed. That's how he's wired to handle situations.

If you hurt Tony or something Tony cares about deeply, you're in trouble. It may happen slowly, some time down the line. Tony may not know he's going to do it, won't realize he's pushing things in that direction, but he's going to get you. Ralph Cifaretto had pissed him off one too many times. Richie Aprile, if Janice hadn't taken care of him—there's that good old Soprano gene—he would have done it. He has a lot of things inside that drive him to do things even he doesn't understand.

continued on the following spread

ROBE WARRIOR

SOME OF THE COSTUME AND prop elements that define Tony Soprano are visible—the custom suits, the garish print shirts, the cigars. Others are less obvious, such as the heavy ring Tony can often be seen playing with. In Gandolfini's invented backstory, the ring originally belonged to Johnny Boy Soprano, Tony's father, and is a point of pride for the son. "It was the first thing his father bought with the money he made," Gandolfini says. "Whenever Tony's about to hit somebody, he turns it around."

But if you close your eyes and think of Tony, you'll probably see him stalking through the Soprano house, or down the driveway for the newspaper, in his signature robe and slippers. "There's a sound those slippers make scraping across the floor: Gush, gush. That's when I know I'm Tony Soprano," Gandolfini says.

Costume designer Juliet Polcsa specifically chose the heavy terry-cloth robe to highlight Tony's bulk. "He's a big man," she says. "He needed something to carry." And the robe's weight may have had unintended consequences. "That robe is about fifty pounds. It's like a fucking grizzly bear on your back," says Gandolfini. In the early seasons of *The Sopranos* the air conditioning at Silvercup Studios was less than perfect. "I'd be under the lights in this robe, sweating and pissed off. A lot of Tony's anger and irritation in that first season was probably just that: Why can't we fix the fucking air conditioning?"

"YOU BET
SMILE O

continued from the previous spread

Intellectually, Tony knows the difference between right and wrong. He loves his family and his wife. He'd be devastated if anything ever happened to Carmela. When he tells her he's not going to cheat anymore, he probably believes it. But he can't help but feed his own appetites, so he goes out and fucks some girl and then feels guilty. Then the guilt gets turned into something else—anger, depression—and it becomes a constant battle. I mean, he's had to kill his best friend, Pussy. He's killed his friend's son. He's killed his cousin. He's always got to worry about who may put a bullet in *his* head. There's a lot of baggage there. A lot of fucking baggage.

What you see in Tony is that a life of materialism, of constantly feeding on the world, leads to nothing but emptiness. Someone like Paulie Walnuts has his way of life and he is what he is. He can be happy. But Tony is smart enough to know that there should be more, a bigger picture. He sees through all the bullshit around him. So he's empty. That's what eats at him: Why can't I be happy? Even when things are going well, I'm not happy. And there's too much history, too much baggage, for anything to ever really change. There's no way out.

He's really not that different from anybody else."

TER WIPE THAT FF YOUR FACE. "

EDIE FALCO ON

CARMELA SOPRANO

"I THINK THAT, ON SOME LEVEL, CARMELA KNOWS EVERYTHING ABOUT WHAT HER HUSBAND DOES FOR A LIVING. BUT IN ORDER TO LIVE DAY TO DAY, SHE CAN'T SPEND A LOT OF TIME DWELLING ON IT. If she ever sat down and thought about what's going on, she'd have to face the fact that it doesn't jibe with her beliefs—certainly not her religious background, or her love for her children. There are a million reasons why being Tony Soprano's wife doesn't work for her, but it provides a certain level of comfort, so she goes through her day in a kind of nowhere land.

We probably first understood just how aware Carmela is of her situation when she asked her neighbor's sister, Joan Cusamano, to write a college recommendation for Meadow. We hadn't ever seen Carmela take advantage of her position before. When Joan said no, Carmela told her: "I don't think you understand. You are going to write this thing." That's when we really got that she's a mobster's wife.

Carmela is like any mother: fiercely protective and deeply loyal, and she'd do anything to make sure her children's well-being is protected. At the same time, she almost doesn't care what they're doing as long as they say they're happy. If A.J. were ever to work with her husband, she might have to slip into denial about that, too.

She's comfortable flaunting her body. She wears low-cut clothing and lots of jewelry. Carmela is married to a big, powerful man, so I suppose she feels safe doing that. I don't think she's worried someone is going to take advantage if she dresses seductively. She's thought about having affairs. There was the wallpaper guy and Furio and, of course, A.J.'s teacher Mr. Wegler. Being Tony Soprano's wife will always be her Scarlet Letter—but she definitely likes imagining it. I mean, a real Italian man who finds her fascinating and dances with her? Absolutely.

Carmela is smart in her way, but I don't know how much she's ever really challenged herself. She's got her charities and book clubs; once she read *Memoirs of a Geisha* for an entire season. We had that prop onstage forever. Every goddamned scene, the same book!

Over time, we've seen Carmela grow a little. She actually left Tony at one point, which isn't something we would have seen in earlier seasons.

continued on the following spread

NAIL CALL

THERE ARE NUMEROUS WAYS in which Edie Falco's down-to-earth sense of style differs mightily from the high-maintenance look of Carmela Soprano. "Every day I do the show, I spend two hours in hair and makeup," Falco says. "They slather foundation on my face and do up my hair and add all this jewelry. Sometimes I look in the mirror and the Edie voice says, 'My god, I look fucking hideous!'" The most striking difference between actress and character, though, is Carmela's perfect manicure. In fact, after long stretches away from set, the moment that Falco reconnects with Carmela comes when the makeup department applies her fake nails. "They're a very powerful thing, because you can't do anything," she says. "Your hands move differently because you've got these long things on the end of them. You can't button things or dial the phone or anything. Basically you need to leave most of the chores to other people."

continued from the previous spread

Maybe she was testing the boundaries of who she is. It's like when she went to Paris; it was a big deal for her to travel by herself, without Tony and the kids. Or the spec house she's trying to build: She's seeing if she can do it on her own.

But she's so embedded in the world she's in—she's been with Tony for twenty years—that I don't know how much she ever really thinks, *I can fly free.* When she's separated from Tony, she finds it harder than she thinks it will be. Their life together provides her with so much that it's hard for her to walk away.

She's not entirely thrilled to have landed back where she started, but it's a lot like real life: How often do moments of revelatory change really happen to people? I think we can all relate to having impulses to move in certain directions but then not following through on them. Huge change is hard.

Who knows? Maybe if she had been born into a different family, Carmela might have been a really bright, courageous woman."

"THE MINUTE I MET TONY, I KNEW WHO THE GUY WAS. AND I DIDN'T KNOW IF I LOVED HIM IN SPITE OF IT, OR BECAUSE OF IT."

— *CARMELA SOPRANO*

MEADOW SOPRANO

"MORE THAN ANY OTHER CHARACTER, MEADOW HAS HAD THE BEST CHANCE TO GET OUT OF *THE SOPRANOS*'S WORLD, the best chance to start a new life. But it's like that old cliché: The more she tries to get away, the more they pull her back in.

When we first met her, she was a junior or senior in high school and she was planning to get as far away from New Jersey as possible. We'd see her bring home her SAT words in a way that made her feel superior—like she wanted to use words that Carmela wouldn't understand. That was a little of her brattiness coming through.

I think Meadow has known what her family's situation was from a very young age. She may seem okay about it, but it has to have weighed on her. Everybody in the family is in a state of denial, because they don't want to believe that the people they love are capable of horrible acts. I think that's why, in the first few seasons, a lot of people thought Meadow was bratty and bitchy. Any time she argued with her parents, she could say, 'How can you tell me what to do? Look what you did! Look who you are!'

Meadow and Tony did have a confrontation when she called him 'Mr. Mob Boss' and he got in her face. It was an incredibly powerful moment because Meadow is very much like her father. They both view showing emotions as a sign of weakness. But during that face-off, both their facades were down. He looked at her not as his little princess but more like, *Who is this little bitch calling me names?* And she looked at him like, *Who is this bastard telling me how to live my life?*

At one point, Tony told Meadow, 'You're more like me than your mother.' I think she was proud of that but also scared. She probably went up to her room that night and tried to think about how to take that in a good way. Because her father really is the most important person in her life. He's her hero, the person who, no matter how many times they butt heads, would scoop her up and save her if she was ever in danger.

I don't see Meadow becoming one of these Mafia wives, but you never know; when she was with Jackie Jr. and she was in love, nothing mattered. When she knew he was dealing Ecstasy, she started doing it with him. And at his funeral when somebody started bad-mouthing the family in front of an outsider, she leapt to their defense. Same thing when Finn saw Vito Spatafore engaging in oral sex with another man at the construction site and was scared to tell anybody—she sided with the family.

Meadow might not condone her family's actions, but she accepts that there's nothing she can do. She loves them very much. You can't choose your family."

SUPER SUITE

TEN YEARS OF BEING ON the air might not mean a lot to most of *The Sopranos* cast members—a few more pounds here, a little less hair there—but for the show's youngest cast members it's been a lifetime. We've watched Jamie-Lynn Sigler and Robert Iler morph from a sixteen-year-old girl and a pudgy twelve-year-old into young adults.

"Jamie and I talk about how, even when we're fifty we're still going to be known as 'the kids,'" says Iler. "The rest of the cast is still going to think they have to look out for us. I mean, every time I see Tony Sirico, he tells me that I need to eat more."

Like any kids, there's perhaps no better way to chart Meadow's development than through her bedroom. Even though she ostensibly left home years ago, Meadow's room remains a teenage girl's refuge, complete with a collage of friends' photos (the pictures are actually of one of the set decorators), old issues of *Playbill* and the art posters of a young woman testing out her maturity. "She's evolving, but there are still things left over," says Sigler.

THONY SOPRANO JR.

"A.J. IS ONE OF THE FEW CHARACTERS THAT CHANGES EVERY SEASON. WHEN WE MET HIM, HE WAS THIS CLUELESS KID. Then he was a skate punk and a goth kid. He found out he could get away with a lot more than he thought he could. He dropped out of college and was working at Blockbuster. And then he finally seemed like he was ready to start taking on some responsibility.

I think he's very confused.

He grew up with people whom he thought were his family—Uncle Paulie, Uncle Silvio—and as he got older it became clearer and clearer that they're just gangsters. He wondered, *Is this cool? Is this bad?* It's hard for him because obviously he's not the brightest Crayon in the box.

It's not that A.J. is stupid, really. He just has a kind of dumb innocence about him that can make him *seem* stupid. He understands what his father does, but I don't think he really considers that Tony's going out there and killing people with his bare hands. A big part of A.J. is being in a fog all the time.

I don't know any teenager who doesn't sit on their bed and say, at some point, 'I hate my parents', or 'I wish I was somebody else's kid.' A.J. has definitely been through that. Then, when his father got shot by Uncle Junior and was in a coma, he realized how much he loved his family and kind of lost it. Trying to go after his uncle was a big move for A.J., even if it was a dumb idea.

It's hard for A.J. because he's always the youngest one around and, it seems to him, the least important. When he meets Blanca at the construction site, he sees an opportunity to be the most important person in her life and vice versa. I think that made him happy.

He's scared of his father, but a lot less than everybody else. A.J. gets to see Tony at his most vulnerable, when he's walking around in his bathrobe, not when he's beating the shit out of people in the back room of the Bada Bing. There was one scene where Tony throws him up against a wall and A.J. says, 'One day I'm going to kick your fucking ass.' I don't know if any of the other guys would ever say that to Tony. And if they did, I don't think they'd be in the next episode.

You just never know with A.J. One day, he's going around like a tough guy. The next time you see him he might be in bed crying like a baby. It's hard to know what he's going to do with his life.

Sometimes I just want to step outside of my character and smack myself in the face."

SOCKS APPEAL

A.J.'S DOMAIN CONTAINS signs of his various selves—from high school class schedules and old hockey tickets to bottles of Crew cologne and posters of bands like Type-O Negative and Incubus. There are also more unsavory artifacts. "In the second season, there was a scene where I was supposed to be masturbating in my room," says Iler. "One of the set dressers thought that it would be funny to tie the sock A.J. supposedly used to one of the bedposts. So sometimes, if you look closely, you can see A.J.'s jerk-off sock."

Which goes to show that, every once in a while, there's something to be said for less attention to detail.

"THE ONE THING YOU NEED TO KNOW ABOUT JANICE IS THAT SHE'S A SURVIVOR. SHE'S A CHAMELEON. WHATEVER SHE NEEDS TO DO TO SURVIVE, SHE'S GOING TO DO. Whoever she needs to be, she's going to be. She looks at the world and thinks, *Poor me. Nobody's taking care of me. I have to do it myself.* She's got a lot of her mother in her.

A lot of people look at the things she does and think she's evil, but she's not. She doesn't do things to hurt people on purpose. She stole Svetlana's leg because she needed the money from selling Livia's records, not because she wanted to torture a one-legged girl. She got rid of Bobby Bacala's dead wife's ziti because she needed a husband. Janice is not somebody you'd really want in your life, but at least she's not intentionally mean.

Clearly Janice comes from a family with a lot of psychosis. I think as a child she was abused—not physically abused, but emotionally and verbally abused. There was a lot of dysfunction in that family. So she left home as soon as she could and left Tony with all the responsibility. She did the hippie thing when it suited her. She got married and had a kid when that suited her. Finally, she wasn't twenty or thirty anymore and she was tired of running, so she came home. She didn't want to work anymore. That's another thing about Janice: She's really lazy.

Sex is just another thing to use, just another tool. Ralphie Cifaretto was just another thing to be busy with. But with Richie Aprile—I think there was a real connection there. They had history. He was going to give her what she wanted—a house and money and a nice little life—but I think there was also a real attraction. When she shot him, it all happened in an instant. She thought, *Oh my God, he punched me. Am I in danger? Should I get him before he gets me? Plus, my brother doesn't like him. How does that affect me?* Boom!

Janice doesn't give a shit about Bobby. She just wants to be married. She couldn't care less about his kids. Even when she freaks out at her stepdaughter's soccer game and beats up another mother. If you asked her, she'd *say* it's because she loves them—and she might even believe it. But she's just playing another role.

There are times when we've seen her actually try to be better. Like taking anger-management classes. I think she was sincere about that. But then Tony basically said, 'Fuck you. You're going to be as miserable as I am.' There are times when Janice and Tony really love each other and other times they really hate each other. He knows exactly how to push her buttons. And Janice is one of the few people who isn't afraid of Tony. That's what makes her such a good nemesis for him. She's always got something up her sleeve."

LIP SERVICE

WHEN JANICE SOPRANO arrived home, she was still going by her "Hindu name," Parvati, and dressing like a Seattle hippie. After hooking up with her old flame, Richie Aprile, it didn't take long for her to shed the scarves and sandals in favor of the Mafia Wife look.

One remnant of her former self impossible to shed, however, was the Rolling Stones tattoo imprinted on her décolletage. "It's the symbol of her youth, of her years of rebellion," says Aida Turturro. The famous tongue-and-lips image is perfect in its imperfection; up close, it looks more like something a teenager would draw on the cover of her loose-leaf notebook than the actual logo.

Like Janice's other tattoo, a ring of vines around her ankle, the Stones lips-and-tongue is a fake, applied every shooting day by the makeup department. A huge Stones fan herself, Turturro once met Keith Richards who asked to see her ink. "I was like, 'Oh no! I wish it was real!'" she says. "I would have been so cool."

CHAPTER 4

ON FUCKING, ZITI,

Sau'

PORK

MEAT

...AND FUCKIN' ZITI:

A SHOW WITH LARGE APPETITES

HE'LL DEVOUR EVERYT

"HE'S AN EATER.
ING IN FRONT OF HIM."

THAT'S HOW LORRAINE BRACCO, WHO PLAYS DR. MELFI, DESCRIBES HER CHARACTER'S MOST VOLATILE PATIENT.

Whether it's for blow jobs or *braciole*, steak or strippers, Tony Soprano prowls his domain in a constant state of hunger—at times fighting against his appetites, more often giving in. To varying degrees, the same can be said for nearly every character on a show that turns out to be about consumption, in its many forms, as much as anything else. Here, food is family, but it's also death. Sex is love, but it's also violence. And everybody seems to have a passionate, complicated—not to say dysfunctional—relationship with the things they crave most.

"SO, WHAT? NO FUCKIN' ZITI NOW?"
—A.J. SOPRANO

OF ALL THE CHARACTERS, IT WAS LITTLE Anthony Jr. in *The Sopranos* pilot episode who first gave voice to the multifaceted role food would play on the show. Ziti was hardly the only food in that introductory hour: There were the sausages that Tony grilled in an attempt to bring together his family and his Family. The first-ever casualty of *The Sopranos*, a Czech named Emil Kolar, was killed by Christopher on the butcher's block cutting board at Satriale's Pork Store. To Artie Bucco's dismay, we saw the lengths to which these characters would go to protect their favorite culinary hangout. Not for the last time, the episode ended with a scene of ambivalent family face-stuffing.

That was just the beginning: In coming seasons—to name just a few gastronomically driven developments—we saw Tony trace his panic attacks to the sight of *gabagool*, or sliced Italian red-peppered ham; turns out, he once saw his father cut off a man's pinkie in Satriale's. He and A.J. bonded over ice-cream sundaes. Bobby Bacala (a man actually named for food; specifically salt cod) treasured the memory of his lost wife via a remaining tray of her ziti in the freezer—and Janice Soprano, knowing where the threat to her newfound domestic bliss lay, made him eat it. Vito Spatafore found temporary comfort and acceptance of his homosexuality in a plate of warm "johnny cakes" cooked by a buff New Hampshire firefighter. Carmela flirted with a priest by way of her formidable pasta dinners and, in the fifth season, rekindled her relationship with Tony over adventurous plates of sushi.

We watched Artie Bucco's cooking fall in and out of favor with Carmela and the other ladies who lunch (and Artie get burned by his own kitchen passions). And we kept track of who in the Soprano clan was talking to whom by way of who gathered around the table for Sunday night dinner. Very often, we ended our own Sunday nights by turning off the television with a gnawing wish

that we had some prosciutto in the fridge or that our local red-sauce Italian joint stayed open past 10 P.M.

Of course, there's a robust tradition of food making appearances in mob dramas—from the grapefruit that James Cagney shoves in his moll's face to *The Godfather*'s cannoli and *Goodfellas*'s prison feasts. Healthy portions (if not necessarily healthy food) are practically essential to a show that aims to accurately capture the flavor of Italian-American life. "I don't believe it's a stereotype to say that food is very important to Italians. They've developed one of the world's great cuisines because of it," says David Chase, who remembers food being a dominant subject of his family's conversations.

"Sunday night dinners were huge when I was growing up," says Edie Falco, whose Italian grandmother still hosts traditional Sunday dinner at her home on Long Island. "The kids would be there. Everybody would be drinking cheap wine and eating Grandma's meatballs. It's where I felt loved and well fed."

THERE'S ALWAYS SOMETHING PREDATORY ABOUT THE GUSTO WITH WHICH TONY SETS ABOUT GORGING ON THE WORLD AROUND HIM.

But as much as food means comfort and family on *The Sopranos,* it's hard to avoid its darker significance. Just ask Richie Aprile, whose body was disassembled like a side of beef in the back room at Satriale's, about the connection between meat and murder. Carmela, you sometimes feel, would rather dish out another plate of ziti than engage in actual conversation—whether it's getting to the bottom of what's troubling her kids, or confronting Tony. "That's why Italians are so fat," says Drea de Matteo. "They eat instead of talking to each other." And it's impossible to watch Tony and Pussy tuck into thick steaks in Season Two's "From Where to Eternity" without being vividly reminded by every juicy bite that they're celebrating having just killed a man in cold blood. There's always something predatory about the gusto with which Tony sets about gorging on the world around him. Something tragic, too. Not for nothing did the Greeks and Romans invent a version of hell that included denizens doomed to eternal hunger. Watching Tony pace restlessly through his world, you are always aware that the void he's trying to fill goes far deeper than the stomach, and that all the osso buco in the world isn't going to be enough to fill it.

"Everything you do, you do over food," says Steven Schirripa about Italian-American life. "If you and I get together, it's not going to be over green tea."

NUOVO VESUVIO'S DINING ROOM

With its murals of Mount Vesuvius and Naples, fancy stemware, and flowing tablecloths, Nuovo Vesuvio is obviously Artie Bucco's attempt to impress his clientele. "He wants there to be an Italian flavor, so Tony and his friends feel comfortable," says set decorator Janet Shaw.

ARTIE BUCCO

"ARTIE IS A GUY WHO STRUGGLES WITH THE EXPECTATIONS THAT HE HAS OF HIMSELF. HE'S GOT A SELF-IMAGE PROBLEM. He's not the man he thinks he should be, and it eats away at him. I think he could probably benefit from going into therapy.

He's the nervous type. He's always anxious. He can't just come in and do his thing and then leave. He's always got to be like, 'Hey guys. I'm here. It's Artie.' He's the guy who always talks too much, because he's not sure what to say. It's like he's trying to make up for something.

Part of him is happy with the life choice he made, going into the family business. But another part of him would love to be in Tony's world. He wants the chicks. He wants the power. He wants to be admired. He wants to be recognized and loved and feared. He wants all those things, for sure. But he's not dumb. He recognizes that a lot of these guys who were his customers are no longer alive. He doesn't want to get shot.

I think that Artie's family was very traditional Italian. He probably grew up hearing his parents saying, 'You're not like these people, these mobsters. You'll go to college. You'll become a great chef. You'll run an honest business.' Not that they wouldn't take two or three pigs off the back of a truck now and then. Not every single thing they did was honest.

I imagine that his father and Johnny Soprano, Tony's dad, had a similar relationship. Artie admires Tony, and Tony's always accepted Artie and respected him in a way. That's how he can get away with things like pointing a gun at Tony or throwing food at him. When they fight, it's almost like brothers. They can say anything they want, even punch each other, but they love each other. I don't know if he realizes that if he was ever a real threat to Tony that would probably be the end. It's a hard thing to believe that your friend would kill you."

HAIRY SITUATION

SOMETIMES AN ACTOR'S choices can come back to haunt him. So it is with Artie Bucco's signature mustache. "I brought that in and I've regretted it ever since," laughs John Ventimiglia. "I mean, a mustache? What the hell is that?"

Still, it's hard to deny that Artie's slightly outdated facial hair suits his nervous, striving personality—a flat note hit by a pianist who's just trying too hard. "Artie is never sure exactly how he's supposed to present himself. The mustache is like something he saw in a movie when he was a kid and thought was cool. Maybe his grandfather had one or some cool kids at school," Ventimiglia says.

Given his view of the Bucco look, it's lucky for Ventimiglia that he can quickly regrow the mustache whenever it's needed. "It's just a thin 'stache," the actor says. "I can shave and then get it back within five days or so." He shakes his head, still consumed with rueful contempt for poor Artie's style choice: "He probably thinks it makes him look less bald. Of course it really makes him look more bald."

SEASON 6   EPISODE 6   TITLE   LIVE FREE OR DIE

"Life's not fair. But somehow I believed
my dad about honest work."

ATTRIBUTION   —ARTIE BUCCO

HELL'S KITCHEN:
HOW TO FEED THE FAMILY

F OR THE FOOD ON *THE SOPRANOS* TO CARRY so much weight, both literally and figuratively, it helps to believe that the food is really as good as it looks. The person in charge of that is prop master Diana Burton.

For an average Soprano family dinner, Burton will procure as many as twenty identical trays of baked ziti for Carmela to pull out of the oven and bring to the table. An additional huge batch is

reserved for replenishing actors' plates between takes. Usually such meals arrive ready-made from caterers and are kept warm on burners near the set.

Beverages present their own set of challenges. If a scene involves pouring red wine, for instance, the bottle's label may be stained after each pour, requiring replacements. The props department has its own bottling machine for just such eventualities. Since drinking alcohol on set can make for long workdays (or short ones, depending on the actors' tolerance), Burton has spent many hours in search of the perfect facsimile wine. Grape juice looks best on camera, she says, but can be too sweet and stain the teeth; food coloring and water wreaks less dental havoc but lacks a certain depth of hue. Whiskey causes similar problems; of the various substitutes Burton has tried, James Gandolfini prefers iced tea or watered down Coca-Cola as a stand-in for Tony's glasses of Scotch.

If the primary focus is on making the food look good, making sure it actually tastes good runs a close second. "Almost any other show I watch, the actors are just playing with their food. But food is

such a big part of our show that we really try to make them want to eat it," Burton says. To that end, she takes care to buy quality ingredients. Some days, she even makes the Sunday "gravy" herself, from her grandmother's recipe. For those actors who may be dieting, she provides a low-carb or –calorie option with every fictional meal.

For all that, the actors have to be careful. Falco, like most of the cast, says that she quickly learned not to overdo it. Her costar, however, has never quite gotten the message. "Jim just eats," Falco says, laughing. "He eats in rehearsal. He eats between takes. I'm watching and I just know by the fourth take he's going to be sick. I'm like, 'Just *pretend*.'"

Tony Sirico, who plays Paulie Walnuts, is more sympathetic. "It's real good, the food," he says. "I once needed to eat eight *braciole* for one scene. Let me tell you something, if you're going to eat eight *braciole*, it *better* be good."

Artie was a victim in his own kitchen when Benny shoved his hand in boiling spaghetti sauce (left). His wife, Charmaine (right), remained by his side.

DIANA BURTON'S GRANDMA AGGIE'S SUNDAY GRAVY

When the spirit strikes her, prop master Diana Burton will use this traditional recipe—handed down from her grandmother Agnes "Aggie" V. Buckley—to furnish the Soprano Sunday dinner.

2 28 oz. cans crushed tomatoes
1 6 oz. can tomato paste
6 whole peeled garlic cloves
6 bay leaves
1 tbsp. dried fennel
1 tbsp. dried oregano
Pinch of red pepper flakes
1/4 cup extra-virgin olive oil
Pinch of sea salt
1/4 cup locatelli cheese, plus additional to use as topping.

In a heavy-bottomed pot or skillet, combine all ingredients except cheese, plus two cups of cold water. Over medium flame, bring to a boil then reduce heat and simmer for at least two hours, stirring occasionally and adding water, as necessary.

Just before serving add 1/4 cup of grated cheese and stir. Remove bay leaves and garlic and serve over pasta with additional grated locatelli on the side.

GABAGOOL: Phonetic for sliced cappicola, a spicy boiled ham. Used more generally for a variety of sliced cold cuts.

BACCALA: Italian for dried salt cod.

BRACIOLE: Rolled beef stuffed with vegetables, breadcrumbs, and cheese and cooked in tomato sauce. Similar to French roulade.

MOOZADELL': Italian-American for mozzarella cheese.

PROCIUTT': Italian-American for prosciutto, Italy's famous cured ham, the best of which comes from the region of Parma.

THE TELLTALE

GRAVY: Old school Italian-American for tomato sauce, particularly the long-simmered, homemade variety made with meat, i.e. Sunday gravy.

OSSOBUCO: A heavy dish of veal shanks braised with vegetables.

'SHCAROLE: Italian-American for escarole, a bitter leafy green used in southern Italian soups and stews. Also slang for "money."

MANIGOTT': Italian-American for manicotti, long, tubular pasta stuffed with ricotta cheese and covered in sauce.

SHFOOYADELL': Classic, many layered Neapolitan pastry, filled with sweet ricotta cheese.

GABAGOOL:

THE SOPRANOS FOOD GLOSSARY

SEX AND *THE SOPRANOS*

"THESE GUYS ARE LIVING IN ANOTHER CENTURY."
—ROSALIE APRILE

THE ROLE OF SEX ON *THE SOPRANOS* IS NO less ambiguous and often even darker than the role of food. Whatever your parents may have told you about "when a man and a woman love each other very much," you're unlikely to see much of that here. Whether it's Richie Aprile screwing Janice Soprano while holding a gun to her head, Ralphie Cifaretto beating his stripper girlfriend to death after impregnating her, or Carmela's understanding that for her to satisfy her own sexual wanderlust would mean a literal death sentence for whomever she was with—sex on the show is more often than not tied up with blood and power.

Above all, it's a man's world. Having a *goomara*, or mistress, is so commonplace that Bobby Bacala is roundly mocked for choosing to go without. (The term *goomara* comes from the

---

WHATEVER YOUR PARENTS MAY HAVE TOLD YOU ABOUT "WHEN A MAN AND WOMAN LOVE EACH OTHER VERY MUCH," YOU'RE UNLIKELY TO SEE MUCH OF THAT HERE.

Italian *comare,* or godmother.) The very notion of expending effort on a woman's pleasure is a source of derision and humiliation—so much so that Uncle Junior dumps his *goomara* for blabbing that he went down on her. (Secretly, it seems, all the guys do it, though perhaps they congratulate themselves more than is strictly deserved.) Meanwhile, reciprocal oral attention barely counts as cheating.

Not surprisingly, Janice is one of the few *Sopranos* women who seize the sexual reins, though even she gets her power from becoming whatever her partner du jour is looking for. After the gun business with Richie, she has no trouble turning dominant for Ralphie, who, it seems, goes in for a little pain. ("Last week he told

Like any couple, Christopher and Adriana had their ups and downs. Unfortunately, the ups usually took place while they were both high and the downs included him sitting on her dog and having her killed.

THE BACK ROOM AT THE BADA BING

While the front room of the Bada Bing is filmed on location at a strip club in New Jersey, the hangout in back—with its pool table, porn posters, and twin desks for Tony and Silvio—is constructed at Silvercup Studios.

me to rub his dick raw with a cheese grater," reports Ralphie's *goomara,* Valentina.) What Janice might do for Bacala, meanwhile, is mostly left offscreen.

Tony, of course, has had his own string of affairs. Why they seem to all involve dark-haired, stubborn, and slightly crazy women is a subject perhaps best left for Dr. Melfi's office. What's amazing is that, by the reduced standards of the Bada Bing, he almost qualifies as an enlightened male. When Vito Spatafore is outed as gay, Tony wishes he could live and let live. (It doesn't hurt that Vito has been an excellent earner.) And, for sporadic periods, he genuinely does try to stay faithful to Carmela—or at least he feels guilty about failing.

Still, this is a world of sexual politics with a very distinct code: When Assemblyman Ron Zellman takes up with Tony's Russian ex-*goomara* Irina, it's clear that nothing good lies ahead for the politician—despite the fact that Tony seems to give his approval.

"When that story came up in the writers' room, I said 'This is going to end up with this guy getting beat with a belt. It doesn't matter what Tony says, you can't do that with these guys. It cannot end well,'" says writer and executive producer Terence Winter, who eventually wrote just that scene for the Season Four episode "Watching Too Much Television."

"One of the other writers asked, 'Isn't there a statute of limitations?'" Winter says. "I said, 'Yeah. Eternity. Just find another girl.'"

Frequent director and actor Steve Buscemi remembers the scene that leads up to Tony's decision to beat up Zellman. Tony is driving in his SUV and is overwhelmed by emotion when the song "Oh, Girl," by The Shi-Lites comes on the radio. "You see this little smile come across his face as though he's thinking, *I know what's going to make me feel better,*" says Buscemi. "He wants to do the right thing, but he thinks, *Fuck it.*"

In other words, Tony's appetites win out again.

IT'S A MAN'S WORLD...THE VERY NOTION OF EXPENDING EFFORT ON A WOMAN'S PLEASURE IS A SOURCE OF DERISION AND HUMILIATION.

TONY'S *GOOMARAS*: WHO'S WHO?

IRINA PELTSIN was Tony's alluring Russian *goomara* during the show's first two seasons. When Tony refused to leave his wife and children, Irina attempted suicide. It was Irina who told Carmela that Tony was cheating on her with Svetlana, initiating Carmela and Tony's separation.

VALENTINA LA PAZ was originally Ralph Cifaretto's *goomara,* until she and Tony meet at Hesh's stable. All was well until she began to push Tony to become more serious and Tony informed her he was going back to Carmela. Valentina was badly burned when her robe accidentally caught fire while cooking eggs.

SVETLANA KIRILENKO first appeared as Livia's nurse in Season Two. When Tony let Svetlana stay at the house after Livia died, Janice accused her of stealing a crate of records. Although Svetlana insisted that they were a gift from Livia, Janice retaliated by stealing Svetlana's prosthetic leg.

GLORIA TRILLO met Tony in the waiting room of Dr. Melfi's office. Though intriguingly strong and independent on the surface, Gloria suffered from severe bipolar illness. Tony was infuriated when Gloria showed up at his house ostensibly to talk to Carmela about a new car. After they broke up, Gloria hanged herself in her apartment.

CHAPTER 5

"WHATEVER HAPPENED
THE STRONG,

TO SILENT TYPE?"

PLUMBING *THE SOPRANOS* SUBCONSCIOUS

"PAIN AND TRUTH? K FROM NEW JERSEY."

It's become as iconic a configuration as two dancers about to tango, or boxers squaring off in the ring: These two people in those two chairs in this one room. No matter what else happens in *The Sopranos* world—action and chaos and murder and sex—we've always found ourselves back here, within these curved walls, the Robert Graham statues looking impassively on, the tissue box poised in the center like an oversize chess piece, as it was in the beginning:

"A GUY WALKS INTO A PSYCHIATRIST'S OFFICE...."

THAT, OF COURSE, WAS THE ORIGINAL HOOK of *The Sopranos*: A mobster, suffering from panic attacks and a midlife crisis, goes to see a shrink and ends up on Prozac. That this was the perfect story for the uneasy, undersatisfied, overmedicated end of the millennium was confirmed by the fact that *Analyze This*, a feature film on the same theme, was released the same year. ("C'mon it's a fucking comedy!" protests Tony when someone compares the Harold Ramis film to his situation.)

An even better measure of the current universality of therapy and therapeutic language came when Tony finally admitted to his crew that he was seeing Dr. Melfi. Rather than the death sentence he once feared—with the fellow mobsters worrying he'd spill trade secrets—the revelation mainly draws shrugs. Paulie Walnuts, of all people, admitted that he, too, once saw a therapist, for his "anger issues." Even Irina, Tony's Russian *goomara*, is reading *Chicken Soup for the Soul*. (Tony suggests she instead pick up *Tomato Sauce for Your Ass*. "It's the Italian version," he says.)

"With today's pharmacology, no one needs to suffer with feelings of exhaustion and depression," said Dr. Melfi in the pilot episode, neatly outlining the promise of antidepressants. Little did she know the depth of the therapeutic challenge that lay ahead.

Over the years, we watched as Tony lurched his way through therapy, quitting and then coming back, self-medicating as he saw fit, edging toward breakthrough revelations and then backing off. All in all, it's been a fairly accurate depiction of the groping, circuitous, one-step-forward-two-steps-back process that therapy often is.

Such verisimilitude is hardly an accident. "Of course, we've all been in therapy," says writer-producer Diane Frolov. Adds her husband and writing partner, Andrew Schneider, "Try finding a writer that *hasn't* been."

"We all come to it with at least some sense of what the process is like," agrees Terence Winter. That level of experience has allowed the writing team to rely far more on instinct and experience than medical journals or case histories. David Chase once described the theme of the second season partly as being "plateau therapy," in which Tony struggled to deal with the breakthroughs he encountered with Dr. Melfi in Season One.

But that doesn't mean that Tony's progress could necessarily be mapped using a psychiatry textbook. Other than an informal peutic progress. Another member of the *Slate* panel, Dr. Glen O. Gabbard, published a book, *The Psychology of the Sopranos*, with such chapters as "Bada Being and Nothingness," and once admitted to an "intensive transference" (shrink-speak for "crush on") to Dr. Melfi in front of a gathering of colleagues.

Certainly the chance to watch a fictionalized member of their profession who is neither a pompous ass nor a sinister Freudian—and has nice legs, to boot—has helped such widespread transference. And *The Sopranos* seems to have been good for business; Chase says he's heard reports of macho guys, if not necessarily made guys, suddenly showing up in psychiatrists' offices as *The Sopranos*'s popularity surged. "I think there are probably men out there whose wives saw the show and said to them, 'You know what? You're really unhappy and I'm tired of listening to you. You should get your ass to a therapist,'" he says.

Perhaps the ultimate professional tribute to *The Sopranos* take on therapy came when Lorraine Bracco was invited to speak, along with *The Sopranos* writers Robin Green and Mitchell Burgess, at a meeting

"I THINK TONY SEES THERAPY AS A CHANCE TO SIT WITH AN ATTRACTIVE, EDUCATED ITALIAN-AMERICAN WOMAN WHO LISTENS TO EVERYTHING HE SAYS..."

contact at Dartmouth University in the early seasons—to provide technical details on medications, dosages, etc.—the closest thing to a psychiatric consultant the show has employed has been the woman on whom Chase based Dr. Melfi's character, a Los Angeles therapist named Lorraine Kaufman who has occasionally provided the writers with her analytic profiles of Tony and other characters. For the most part, the course of Tony's therapy has gone wherever the show's plot has required it to go, rather than following a particular therapeutic path.

"We just go from our guts," says Winter. "It's kind of scary because we have therapists coming up to us and saying, 'God, you got it so right. It sounds perfect.'"

Indeed, professional analysts embraced *The Sopranos* from the very beginning. "It's the best representation of the work we do that has ever been on film or television," one Dr. Philip Ringstrom of the Institute of Contemporary Analysis told *The New York Times* in 2001. Ringstrom was one of four therapists who dissected each episode of the third season for the online magazine *Slate* and once made a presentation to the American Psychological Association on how Tony's need to protect his family secrets impacted his thera-

of the American Psychoanalytic Association. "I told them that I was very thankful," says Bracco, "but that they were completely crazy."

"SOMETIMES COMIN' HERE FEELS LIKE TAKING A SHIT."
—TONY SOPRANO

I THINK TONY SEES THERAPY AS A CHANCE to sit with an attractive, educated Italian-American woman who listens to everything he says and doesn't nag him too much," says Chase. "It's peaceful in there."

If that sounds like a cynical view of a highly regarded academic profession, it's indicative of *The Sopranos*'s ambivalent view of the psychiatric profession. Professional therapists may love the show, but it's never been at all clear that the show loves them back. After all, despite occasional breakthroughs and periods of contentment, the process has hardly solved Tony's problems or made him a happier man. "Overall, I think that therapy can be a beneficial thing," says Chase. "But most therapists will let you keep coming back as long as you want. You never reach the end. As great as it can be, it's a whack-off. Tony himself has said it: The people who really need therapy are little kids in Afghanistan who are having their legs blown off, not some guy who feels bad because his mother served him the wrong kind of cutlets."

What is undeniable is that therapy has been of great benefit to *The Sopranos* writers, providing a narrative anchor and ongoing storyline that spans six seasons. It also gives the writers a periodic chance to take a break from the action, step out of the story, and assess what's going on, really. "It's our Greek chorus," says James Gandolfini. "In a very clever way it eliminates the need for voice-over."

"At their most naked, those scenes are where we can have Tony look into the camera and say what he's feeling," adds Chase.

On a show where people almost never say what they really mean, this is a valuable tool, though Chase believes that, over time, the audience has almost begun to do Dr. Melfi's work for her. "There's been a learning curve. It used to be Tony would say something to Carmela and then, with Melfi, explain that he meant the opposite," Chase says. "Now, I think the audience has figured that out. In some ways, we almost don't need Tony in therapy anymore."

"TWO YEARS AGO, I THOUGHT RICO
WAS A RELATIVE OF HIS."
—DR. MELFI

F RETURNING TO DR. MELFI'S PANELED OFFICE sometimes feels like coming home, it's by design. One of the few ironclad dictates that the production imposes on its

changing roster of directors is that there will be no filmmaking funny business in the therapy scenes. "That's really our only rule: You don't move the camera in Melfi's office," says executive producer Ilene Landress. If a director can, say, dramatically push in on Tony's face after a big revelation, it would be making a statement. It would telegraph the story. And then there's an impulse to keep those scenes distinct from the rest of the show. "You don't want to dolly. You don't want the overhead shot or the camera spinning around," says Landress. "We try to keep the camera-work straightforward."

In spite of, or perhaps because of, the intensity of the scenes filmed in Melfi's office, Bracco and James Gandolfini have found ways to relieve the tension. Each scene is shot first with the camera entirely on one character and then shot again (or multiple times more) facing the other way. "The shoots get very complicated," says Bracco. "You're sometimes doing two or three pages of dialogue. So, we try to make the other person laugh when the camera's facing the other way. We're all eight years old."

"SAD IS GOOD. UNCONSCIOUS IS NOT."
— DR. JENNIFER MELFI

Tony and Dr. Melfi in tense discussion.

In one infamous episode, Bracco got fed up with Gandolfini's teasing during her close-ups. "He was scratching his balls and making funny faces, so I decided I would get him," she says. In between takes, she ducked into the makeup trailer, grabbed a long piece of wig belonging to Annabella Sciorra's character, Gloria Trillo, and proceeded to stuff it down her pants, creating an impressive merkin. "When I crossed my legs during the scene, it was just hanging out," she says. "He was so repulsed. It was beautiful."

Another time, a remote-controlled fart machine came into play. Bracco enlisted a prop department worker to place it under the upholstery of Melfi's chair. She remembers, "I set it up in the morning, telling Jimmy how I had eaten Indian food the night before and wasn't feeling well. I wasn't sure I could make it through the day. Then, when the camera turned on him the farts started coming . . . little ones at first and then bigger and bigger. Finally he stood up and basically threw me across the room. He's a big boy."

LORRAINE BRACCO ON

DR. JENNIFER MELFI

"JENNIFER MELFI IS A FIFTY-TWO-YEAR-OLD WOMAN WHO HAS A SON, AN EX-HUSBAND, AND ONE FASCINATING PATIENT.

Melfi is a lonely woman. She's married to her work. She's worked hard to get where she is—grew up in a working-class neighborhood, went to Tufts University, spent ten years getting her degree—and she's proud of that. And I think she thinks she's really helping Tony. She believes that there is a space for a man like him in therapy. That's always been the question: If Adolf Hitler came in and wanted to undergo psychotherapy, would you turn him away? Melfi's answer is 'No. I wouldn't.'

It's an intimate relationship. Therapy always is very intimate. But I can't ever see them falling into bed with each other, thank God. Tony has a problem with her because she's so much smarter than he is. He's not used to that in a woman. With her it's not going to be about sex. That's not what's happening. He's tried a few times, but he's never succeeded. And yet he's come back. That's how you know he has a lot of respect for her.

Still, Melfi knows what kind of animal is in front of her. She has to keep the lines drawn. Because Tony will devour anything that he can. He'll take it. He'll rape it. He'll rob your money. He'll rob your soul. She knows all this.

There was one moment when she was tempted to be corrupted by him. This was after she was raped in the parking garage and had to decide whether to let Tony get revenge for her. She was really pushed to her limit then. She was one second away. Honestly, I couldn't understand that when I first got the script. I said, 'Why are you hurting her? Out of everybody? Why would you hurt the only decent person in *this* world?' But then I read the last scene, when Melfi decides that she can't do it, even though this man hurt her so badly. She was tempted—who wouldn't be? But she was going to have to eat it. She wasn't going to become a gangster. She wasn't going to become him.

Because if Melfi becomes Tony, where are we all going?"

GAM THEORY

PLAYING DR. MELFI PRESENTS a unique acting challenge for Lorraine Bracco. While other actors get to move around a bit—interacting and drawing inspiration from lots of various characters, props, sets, and locations—Bracco has spent the vast majority of her screen time in one office and the vast majority of that time sitting down. (As a kind of cruel joke, when Melfi does get to leave her office it's usually to visit her own shrink in yet another psychiatrist's office.) Bracco had never even been to the Satriale's Pork Store set in Kearny, New Jersey, until a script read-through happened to be scheduled there during Season Six.

Thanks to the static nature of her surroundings, we've always had ample time to see Bracco's excellent legs. "Sometimes we dress her in slacks or a suit, but the male side of the show appreciates the days we use a skirt," says costume designer Juliet Polcsa, who brings a chair into the fitting room for Bracco's fittings to better monitor how high those skirts will rise during the therapy scenes.

Bracco herself doesn't look forward to the skirt days because of what she has to wear underneath them: "I despise pantyhose," the actress says. "I can't stand them." But, she says, Melfi would never go bare-legged. "Not only because she's professional but because she could never show Tony her legs. If she gives him an inch, he's going to take a yard. If she gives him even that little opening, she's a goner."

DR. MELFI'S OFFICE

For all its calming tones and womblike curves, Dr. Jennifer Melfi's office has been the site of some of *The Sopranos*'s most quietly wrenching scenes. The office has changed little over the seasons, though careful viewers will note that Melfi's signature Robert Graham statues (on loan from a collector) do rotate.

THE SOPRANOS DREAM SEQUENCES

"YOU KNOW, DOUCHE BAG, I REALIZE I'M DREAMING."
—TONY SOPRANO

TALKING FISH. ORNERY GYM TEACHERS. Horses (or is it 'whores'?) in the house. Clown cars. Lots and lots of dead people. Annette Bening. Such is the stuff that *The Sopranos* dreams are made of.

Dreams have been a part of the show's vocabulary since the very first episode, when Tony told Dr. Melfi about a dream in which he tries to smoke his own penis as a cigar before a duck flies off with it in its beak. "Some people love the dreams and some people hate them, but they're part of the 'franchise,'" says David Chase. "We do come by our dream sequences honestly. You don't see Don Corleone's dreams or Henry Hill's dreams, but neither of them was seeing a therapist. Dreams and interpreting dreams are a big part of therapy."

Dreams on the show often reveal truths that the dreamer would prefer not to face. In "Funhouse," the finale of Season Two, a bad Indian meal (or Artie Bucco's mussels marinara) sends Tony into a feverish dream state in which he comes to realize that Big Pussy has betrayed him. ("Sooner or later you've got to face facts," the aforementioned fish, a tilefish by the looks of it, intones in Pussy's voice.) Several seasons later, in "The Test Dream," Tony checks into the Plaza Hotel and dreams—despite being distracted by visions of having sex with Charmaine Bucco, enacting scenes from *The Godfather,* and much else—that he's forgotten to do something very important. It's a version of the classic dream in which one shows up for a test unprepared, or naked, except that the test facing Tony seems to be whether he'll kill his cousin Tony Blundetto and prevent a looming war with the New York Family.

Tony isn't the only dreamer forced to face uncomfortable facts. After her rape, Dr. Melfi dreamed of a snarling rottweiler attacking her rapist, a thinly veiled fantasy of allowing Tony to take revenge for her. And it was while asleep in Paris that Carmela allowed herself to consider the notion that perhaps Adriana La Cerva didn't exactly sail happily off into the sunset.

As in real dreams, some elements of *The Sopranos* dreams are easily decipherable. (Tony's obsession with Cooper leads to *High Noon* appearing on a TV screen.) Others are more obscure. (In "Funhouse," is Tony setting himself on fire out of guilt, avoidance, or just because the Indian meal has left him feverish in real life?) And still others seem simply random. (What the hell is Bening doing in "The Test Dream"?)

The Sopranos writers insist that when concocting dream sequences they rely on their own subconscious, rather than any particular symbology or "Book of Dreams." It was only *after* envisioning a talking fish, for instance, that Chase realized the obvious connection to "sleeping with the fishes," which, of course, Pussy is about to do. In "The Test Dream," Tony finds himself out to dinner with the family of Meadow's fiancé, Finn. (He's presumably never met his future in-laws, so his mind casts Vin Makazian, the corrupt cop who committed suicide in Season One, and Bening in the roles of Finn's mother and father.) At the table, Tony suddenly begins losing his teeth. Says Matt Weiner, who wrote the episode with Chase, "It's all about embarrassment. He has anxiety about meeting Finn's parents, about sending his daughter off with regular people."

Chase sometimes worries that the dream sequences aren't *organic enough.* "We try to be honest and really take them from the

Big Pussy's betrayal, and death, pervades Tony's dreams.

dark subconscious or even unconscious place, but sometimes they wind up carrying too much narrative weight. They deliver too much information," he says. "If the writer knows that eventually Melfi is going to have to say 'Do you think this means this or that?' it's probably going to affect what he puts in the dream."

At least one *Sopranos* dream came directly from real life; in fact, the very first one. John Patterson, a frequent director of the show who passed away in 2005, had told his longtime friend Chase about his own penis-as-cigar dream. "Trying to smoke his own penis, I always found that very funny," Chase says, laughing. "I only had to add the duck."

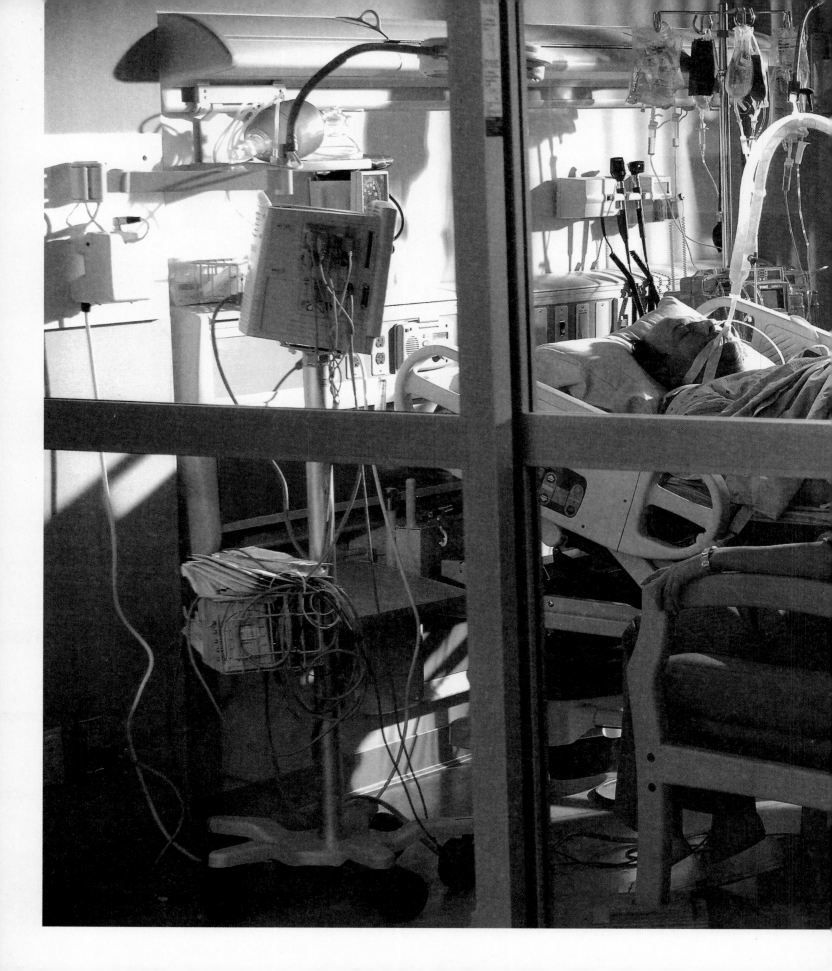

SEASON 6 | EPISODE 2 | TITLE JOIN THE CLUB

"Tony Soprano is not going to die. I don't know
what everybody is talking about."

ATTRIBUTION   —A.J. SOPRANO

CHAPTER 6

"GOT MYS

ELF A GUN"

THEFT, MURDER, AND OTHER ASSORTED
VIOLENT TENDENCIES

ENT CONSULTANT."

THAT WAS TONY SOPRANO'S ANSWER WHEN, IN HIS VERY FIRST THERAPY SESSION, DR. MELFI HESITANTLY ASKED WHAT HE DID FOR A LIVING.

Of course, she knew exactly what that was code for. Or did she? Either way, the audience knew that, whatever else *The Sopranos* was going to be—family story, suburban story, psychiatric story, American story—it was also going to be a mob story, complete with all the pleasures, guilty and otherwise, that venerable genre provides. We would have gunplay and piles of cash, baroque induction ceremonies and ancient codes of honor, the horror of bloody violence and the allure of ruthless wise guys living outside the law.

THE SOPRANOS HAS PROVIDED ALL OF THOSE things and more, but rather than the mythological Mafia Golden Age depicted in *The Godfather* or even the swinging seventies of *Goodfellas*, the show has also aimed to depict organized crime as it exists today. That's a world in which, with no small thanks to those iconic movies, the once secret society, "our thing," has long since been shared with the rest of the world. It's a world where the twin scourges of drugs and RICO (the Feds' ability to try mobsters for conspiracy) put lie to whatever myths of loyalty, honor, or *omertà* still survive; it's one thing to honor a code of silence when you're facing five years in prison; the prospect of going away for life, it seems, has a way of loosening even the most loyal of tongues. Tony may be on to something when he frets that "the best is over."

CHRISTOPHER:

"GARBAGE IS OUR BREAD AND BUTTER."

TONY:

"WAS."

NONE OF WHICH MEANS, OF COURSE, THAT there aren't enormous piles of money to be made as the boss of northern New Jersey. Exactly how much Tony is worth has always been left somewhat vague—even Carmela, when she considered getting a divorce, had trouble coming up with an exact number—so as not to get in the way of the story. Between $5 million and $6 million is writer Terence Winter's best estimate—some of it in real estate (he owns Satriale's and at least part of the Bada Bing), some holed up in offshore accounts (facilitated by Russian mobster Slava), much of it in wads of cash stashed in various places, including, of course, the duck-food bin out in the backyard.

What we do know is that Tony sits at the very peak of a large pyramid that follows the real-life structure of an organized crime family. Each level of the pyramid kicks up a portion of its earnings to the level above—from street thugs to soldiers to captains to the

"SHIT RUNS DOWNHILL, MONEY GOES UP."

— TONY SOPRANO

Tony and Ralphie visit Pie-Oh-My.

boss himself. Even if you accept as a given that each person in the chain is lying to the next about how much they really earned, the sums add up pretty quickly. And, in any event, hard times fall hardest on the men at the bottom, since it's the boss who sets what in another business would be called "revenue projections." Good earners, the guys who keep those envelopes of cash fat each week, buy themselves a lot of leeway; consistent earning is what makes Tony so hesitant to lose Vito Spatafore and Ralph Cifaretto. Those who hand over thin envelopes, meanwhile, do so at their peril, as an increasingly panicked Paulie understands when he resorts to knocking over old ladies to get the tribute Tony expects.

As to where the money itself comes from, first and foremost there's illegal gambling. Even with state-run lotteries and casinos in nearly every state, estimates on the size of the illegal sports betting business run anywhere from $100 to $400 billion per year, most of it moving through bookies.

Hijacking trucks and fencing whatever happens to be inside—suits, stereos, fish, vitamins—is another profitable area for

both the Soprano Family and their real-world counterparts. (Richie Aprile once ruminated that small, nonperishable items like scissors were the perfect haul: "Everybody wants one, nobody has a fuckin' idea how much they cost.") Then there are such traditional mob businesses as garbage and construction—both of which rely upon contract rigging and union corruption. Tony happens to be in tight with Jersey's Joint Fitters Union. In return for lending his support to such projects as the Newark Esplanade and the "Newark Museum of Science and Trucking," Tony gets a certain number of jobs for his crew. "There are no-show jobs and there are no-*work* jobs," Winter clarifies. "On no-work jobs, you still have to show up." Either way, Tony winds up with a cut.

Same goes for garbage routes, which are set in stone. According to his W2 tax form, Tony works for Barone Sanitation—an arrangement that proved problematic when Dick Barone died and the New

York Family took over the business. The one time he tried actually working on the Barone premises, in the aptly titled Season Two episode "House Arrest," he found the straight life less than entirely satisfying; despite such diversions as starting a betting pool and having sex with a receptionist, he only made it a few days before defying his lawyer's orders and returning to work at the Bada Bing.

At least since Sonny Corleone declared, "There's a lot of money in that white powder," the mob has had a love/hate affair with the drug trade—mostly, it has to be said, love, given dope's vast profit potential. Winter says that Tony probably adopts a "don't ask/don't tell" policy toward his people selling drugs. He is even less concerned by such other unseemly vocations as loansharking and prostitution.

And he is always open to new avenues of opportunity, whether it's taking over an Orthodox Jewish–owned motel, scamming HMOs with charges for fake MRIs, siphoning off Federal Housing and Urban Development grants, or dismantling his friend's sporting goods business and selling off the spare parts—what's known as a "bust out."

All in all, it adds up to a decent income, though, says Winter, it's hard to say how much of it stays in Tony's coffers. "These guys aren't the best money managers," Winter says. "Tony probably pisses a huge amount of his money away."

"IT'S OVER FOR THE LITTLE GUY."
—PATSY PARISI

WHILE MANY TRADITIONAL MOB BUSINESSES still thrive, the modern world has taken its toll. In the Season Six episode "Johnny Cakes," Patsy Parisi and an associate attempted to do what they had surely done a thousand times before: extort protection money from a new neighborhood business. Unfortunately for them, the new business happened to

Tony hides some of his cash in a bag of duck feed.

WE DO KNOW THAT TONY SITS AT THE VERY PEAK OF A LARGE PYRAMID THAT FOLLOWS THE REAL-LIFE STRUCTURE OF AN ORGANIZED CRIME FAMILY.

be a corporate coffee chain. When Parisi asked for a weekly donation to the "North Ward Merchants Protective Cooperative," the manager told him he'd have to clear it through corporate headquarters, in Seattle.

"How would headquarters feel if a brick came through the window?" Patsy's friend asked. "Well," said the perplexed manager, "they've got like ten thousand stores in North America, I don't think they'd feel anything." The mobsters exited, bewildered. "You can't shake down Starbucks," David Chase says, laughing. "No matter how big you think you are, they will roll right over you."

These are the moments when we suddenly realize that the Soprano crew, and even the more powerful New York mobsters, may be the richest, most vicious fish in their tiny pond, but they are mere guppies when it comes to real wealth and real power. Hell, in the age of Enron and WorldCom, they're arguably not even the most despicable thieves in town. Out on the sidewalk, Patsy is the very picture of a mobster whom the world has passed by. His boss, however, has been more attentive to the way the wind blows.

Later in the same episode, Tony sells Caputo's live poultry shop—the very definition of an "old neighborhood" business, and a steady protection payer—to a company no self-respecting wise guy would ever be caught dead patronizing: Jamba Juice.

"TAKE IT EASY, WE'RE NOT MAKING A WESTERN HERE."
—UNCLE JUNIOR

IT'S NO ACCIDENT THAT SUCH TWISTS AND turns of contemporary mob life make their way onto *The Sopranos*. Unlike the show's therapy scenes, with which the writers are allowed a certain freedom of expression, Chase's mandate has always been to stick to the hard facts when it comes to mob life. "In talking therapy, there really isn't any right or wrong, so we can kind of feel our way along," says Winter. "When it comes to crime, David wants precedent. He wants to know something similar has happened in that world before."

SEASON 6 | EPISODE 10 | TITLE MOE 'N JOE

"That selfish prick. I'm sitting here facin' a shitstorm
and all [Tony] can think about is himself?"

ATTRIBUTION   —JOHNNY SACK

To that end, the writers' office contains an extensive library of mob lit—from *The Boys from New Jersey*, about the Lucchese Family's adventures in the Garden State, to *Wiseguys Say the Darndest Things*. Production assistants are also assigned to comb through the *New York Post, Daily News, Newark Star-Ledger,* and other papers each day, clipping out any organized crime-related stories. The clips are then filed in a collection worthy of a newspaper morgue, under such categories as "ID Theft," "Scams," "Gotti," and "Sex Clubs."

Perhaps most important, the show employs a consultant named Dan Castleman. A chief investigator for the Manhattan District Attorney's office, Castleman is on call to answer writers' questions on matters of mob etiquette and legal procedure: How long would Tony be held if he were arrested? If Uncle Junior's under house arrest, how can he go to funerals? Can Johnny Sack smoke in prison? The writers will also call Castleman to ask after new developments in the mob world—scams like the HUD deal, say, or changes in hijacking techniques at the ports.

Usually, says Winter, Castleman's answer is "No"; most mobsters still cling to the old ways and old businesses. "Dan tells us that, for the most part, these guys just sit outside pork stores and eat sandwiches. In some ways, it's actually a pretty dull life."

"THIS MAY COME AS A SURPRISE TO YOU, BUT THESE PEOPLE DID NOT COME HERE TO SEE SOPRANOS KILL EACH OTHER."

—CARMELA SOPRANO

THERE IS ONE AREA IN WHICH *THE SOPRANOS* does exaggerate its view of organized crime and that is in the number and frequency of mob murders—from the very first whacking of Czech garbage scion Emil Kolar to the stabbing and

THOUGH THE SHOW INSISTS ON DEPICTING MURDER IN ALL ITS BLOODY SLOP AND HORROR, KILLING IS REALLY ONLY THE TIP OF THE ICEBERG.

beheading of Fat Dom toward the middle of Season Six, with a long string of bodies in between. "The fact is that it's barely realistic," says Chase. "We've already had triple the number of murders that organized crime ever commits."

Still, there are those in the show's audience who want ever more blood and guts. Throughout the course of the show, whenever the body count dwindled, you could count on the complaints starting to pour in. Chase acknowledges that violence is a vital part of the show—"That's what you go to a gangster picture for: To see people get it"—but he and the other writers have occasionally been taken aback by their viewers' desire for more and more bloody fare. "I've just been amazed at the bloodlust," says writer and co-executive producer Matthew Weiner.

"Some people aren't happy unless you're chopping off someone's head," Chase says. "That would be so easy for us. We could kill a character every week. But what would be the point? If you don't know who these people are, if you have no feeling for them, what difference does it make? It's just a stunt man being hit with fake blood."

In the end, it comes down to the delicate balancing act that has defined *The Sopranos*: How to make you root for, laugh with, and identify with these characters while never losing sight of the fact that they are often doing truly heinous things. That's the joy and the paradox of the gangster genre.

And, though the show insists on depicting murder in all its bloody slop and horror, killing is really only the tip of the iceberg. If you're a decent, hardworking police officer unlucky enough to pull Tony Soprano over for speeding, your life will be ruined. If Paulie happens to notice your business and want a piece, you're trapped. As funny as it might be to watch the guys hanging out in the back room of the Bada Bing, it's hard to

imagine anything scarier than learning that you've attracted their attention.

Indeed, wherever the Soprano business goes, misery tends to follow. When they siphon off HUD subsidies, poor people go without housing. When they open strip clubs, young girls become prostitutes. When they take over construction projects, tax dollars go down the drain. When they feud over gardening routes, poor gardeners get their arms broken. "Organized crime *does* cost society," says Chase.

And yet only few of us would pretend that there isn't something deeply romantic about the gangster life—the very thing that turns us on about mob movies and TV shows. Tony doesn't have to work in an office. He makes tons of money. He has sex with

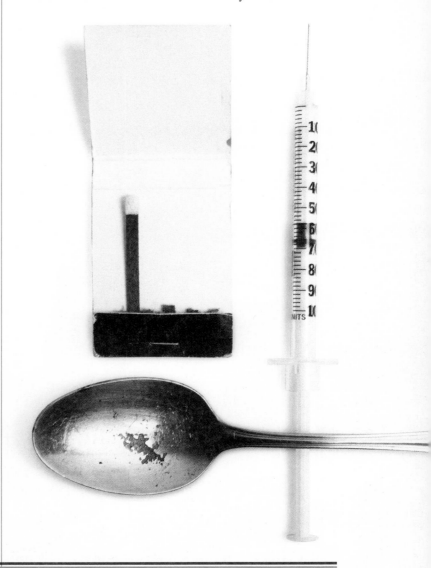

Above: For six seasons, Christopher has struggled to stay clean. Left: Fat Dom is stabbed in the back room of Satriale's shortly after killing Vito.

whomever he wants. If he doesn't like somebody, he can kill him. Looked at in a certain light, he is free in a way that most men only dream of. As the rapper Da Lux proclaims, when they meet in the hospital, "Tony Soprano, original G!"

"On some level, I love Tony Soprano and his guys. Everybody loves the Robin Hood myth," says Chase. "When I read about organized crime it's like, *Yeah! Take it, shoot them! There's bigger motherfucking crooks in the White House and its war profiteers.* It's easy to feel that way."

Certainly that's the disease with which so many "civilian" characters on *The Sopranos* are afflicted—the Davey Scatinos and J.T. Dolans and Artie Buccos and even Special Agent Harrises. They are drawn to Tony and his world like moths to a flame, more often than not with similarly unhappy results.

And it's useful to remember what *The Sopranos* never lets us forget: that Tony Soprano—outlaw, Robin Hood, *capo di capi*—has been in therapy for a decade now, with no sign of stopping or getting closer to some kind of happiness. Freedom, it seems, isn't always what it's cracked up to be. It can even feel like prison.

Trash heaps in Jersey.

TRASH TALK

"I'M IN THE WASTE-MANAGEMENT BUSINESS. EVERYBODY IMMEDIATELY ASSUMES YOU'RE MOBBED UP. IT'S A STEREOTYPE, AND IT'S OFFENSIVE."
—TONY SOPRANO

TONY CAN COMPLAIN ALL HE WANTS, GARBAGE and organized crime have been inextricably linked for decades—almost since the mob's last great monopoly, on booze, was snapped by the repeal of Prohibition. According to *Takedown: The Fall of the Last Mafia Empire* by Rick Cowan, a New York City detective who helped break that monopoly, it was a criminal visionary named Vincent "Jimmy" Squillante who first saw gold in garbage—a service that no business in the metropolitan area could do without. New York and northern Jersey's com-

mercial trash routes were divvied up by the five major Mafia families and their associates by the the mid-1950s and, despite countless investigations and even hearings helmed by Robert and John F. Kennedy, garbage evolved into the mob's "legitimate" business of choice. By 1995, the nationwide waste-management business was estimated at $1.5 billion—a healthy portion of which was made up of a 40 percent "mob tax." And the affiliation isn't limited to the U.S. either; a recent report by the Italian government found that a ring of organized families has an iron grip on that country's waste industry, too.

As *The Sopranos* has demonstrated, controlling garbage routes opens other possibilities, too, whether it's as a cocaine distribution network (as Uncle Junior and Richie Aprile attempt) or as a convenient way to make the remains of a colleague disappear. It's no accident that Christopher's brilliant mob/slasher film *Cleaver* features a protagonist whose body is chopped up and deposited into multiple dumpsters and reanimated at the local landfill. (After much deep dis-

cussion amongst the mobsters Christopher pitches the idea to, it is agreed that the dumpsters would all have to be along the same route to ensure that all the body parts reach the same landfill.)

For all that, the glory days of the mob-run carting business are over. The first major blow to the business came in the 1990s, when the New York cartel was infiltrated by Rick Cowan, an undercover police officer. The investigation, code-named Operation Wasteland, resulted in more than one-hundred indictments and broke the grip of the Families on the metropolitan area's garbage routes.

But the more important and powerful enemy to the mob-controlled garbage cartels were big waste-management corporations. Like Las Vegas casinos and liquor sales before it, there was ultimately too much money in garbage for the business to be left to the wise guys indefinitely. More and more, experts say, giant waste corporations, and their lower fees, have left guys like Tony looking for alternate business opportunities.

THE SLEEVELESS TANK-TOP UNDERSHIRT... A CRUCIAL MOB-GUY ACCESSORY AT LEAST SINCE JAMES CAAN SHOWED HIS OFF IN *THE GODFATHER*.

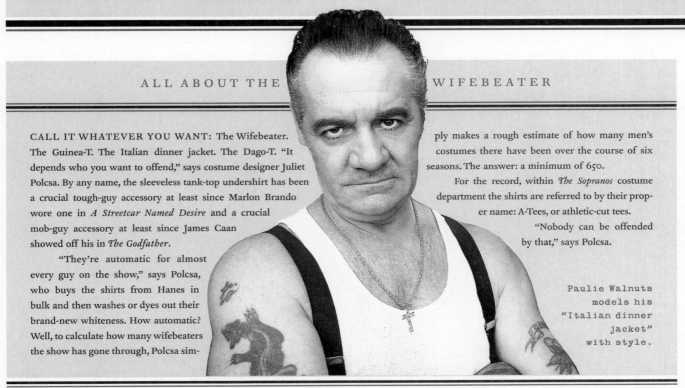

ALL ABOUT THE WIFEBEATER

CALL IT WHATEVER YOU WANT: The Wifebeater. The Guinea-T. The Italian dinner jacket. The Dago-T. "It depends who you want to offend," says costume designer Juliet Polcsa. By any name, the sleeveless tank-top undershirt has been a crucial tough-guy accessory at least since Marlon Brando wore one in *A Streetcar Named Desire* and a crucial mob-guy accessory at least since James Caan showed off his in *The Godfather*.

"They're automatic for almost every guy on the show," says Polcsa, who buys the shirts from Hanes in bulk and then washes or dyes out their brand-new whiteness. How automatic? Well, to calculate how many wifebeaters the show has gone through, Polcsa sim-

ply makes a rough estimate of how many men's costumes there have been over the course of six seasons. The answer: a minimum of 650.

For the record, within *The Sopranos* costume department the shirts are referred to by their proper name: A-Tees, or athletic-cut tees.

"Nobody can be offended by that," says Polcsa.

Paulie Walnuts models his "Italian dinner jacket" with style.

"WHEN WE FIRST MET CHRISTOPHER, HE WAS IN THE MIDDLE OF KILLING A GUY. It was for the business, part of a turf war against rival garbage guys. That was his first kill, and it gave Tony a certain amount of trust in him. He was solidifying his role, making his bones.

Christopher is a relative of both Tony and Carmela's. His father was a legendary mob guy named Dickie Moltisanti. Ultimately, Dickie was probably just a junkie, a low-level mob guy and a shitty father. But in Tony's eyes he was great, a mentor, and Christopher wants to believe that. He wants him to be a hero. Christopher's a guy who's always tried to better himself, despite having a lot of problems. He's battled drug addiction, alcoholism. He's tried to be a screenwriter. He's cursed by being aware enough to know there are other things out there, but not being able to get there. He's filled with a lot of anger.

I think the mob life is becoming harder for Christopher as he gets older. When he was younger—running errands and stuff for Tony—it was romantic. He was making money, getting some respect, and people started to fear him. These things were exciting to him. Now I think he's realized that these things don't make you happy.

I like the fact that Christopher works really hard at whatever he does. He didn't just have an idea like every other guy, he actually sat down and wrote a script. And it's not totally outrageous. He's got a real writer working with him, he could get a star for $100,000, and, worse comes to worst, it will make its money back. I mean, it's not going to be *Citizen Kane*, but there are worse projects out there. I've been in worse projects.

If one wants to take his sobriety seriously, he needs to take a good look at his life and the major players in his life—and Tony is the major player in Christopher's life. Tony's been like a father to him, taken him under his wing, tried to beat some sense into him. But there are times when Christopher hates him. He feels slighted a lot, like Tony never gives him any credit. He spends a lot of time being jealous and angry.

I think Christopher really considered leaving town with Adriana and going into the Witness Protection Program. But Adriana had been lying to him for a long time. He suspected she had slept with Tony. Everything was tainted. The relationship was never going to be what it once was. And then there was that scene when he's on his way over to Tony's house and stops at the gas station. He sees this family and has a vision of what life would be like in Arizona or wherever they would put him. It's like at the end of *Goodfellas*, and he thinks, *I'll just be another schnook.* Christopher was in a no-win situation.

But I think he feels guilty. He's smart enough to know that, in the end, this whole thing is probably going to blow up and maybe he and Adriana should have made a run for it. And he knows that going to Tony, which essentially meant disposing of her, will probably have some spiritual repercussion on some kind of karmic plane. I mean, for the most part, these guys don't age gracefully."

MAN OF SUBSTANCES

DESPITE A STRING OF INTERventions, 12-step programs, and assorted other stabs at sobriety, Christopher has spent much of *The Sopranos*'s six seasons high on one drug or another. To accommodate his various habits, the prop department has developed a bag of tricks: Retractable syringes give the illusion of piercing the skin, right down to a few drops of fake blood flowing back into the needle. A little sugar browns up very much like heroin when heated on a spoon. Inhaling lactose powder is the most innocuous way for actors to simulate snorting coke. As for Christopher's perpetually burning cigarettes-they've been strictly nicotine-free, herbal smokes since Michael Imperioli quit smoking two seasons ago.

DREA DE MATTEO ON

ADRIANA LA CERVA

"AT THE END OF THE DAY, THE THING ABOUT ADRIANA IS THAT
SHE WAS THE ONE PERSON ON THE WHOLE SHOW WHO DIDN'T
HAVE AN AGENDA. SHE'S THE ONLY REAL INNOCENT.

Yes, there were all those perks of being with the made guy. It's like being with a rock
star. But, in the end, it wasn't about the diamonds or the cars and all that stuff. She just really
loved this guy, Christopher. Anything that would excite him would excite her. If he was working in a supermarket and got promoted, she would have been just as proud. She probably
wanted him to succeed at the screenwriting even more than the mob stuff. It was very pure.

If Adriana would have put even a little of the energy into herself that she did into sup-
porting Christopher, she could have made something of her life. Early on, she wanted to be
a music producer, but once she failed at that she was done. She put everything into him. In
a much more primitive way, she was to Christopher what Dr. Melfi is to Tony Soprano.

I think the biggest misconception about Adriana is that she was tough. Her clothes
and some of her gestures make her look tough. But underneath she was probably one of the
most insecure girls in the world. Anytime she would open up to anybody she would get
stabbed. You saw it when she wanted to make friends with her FBI handler. There's a school
of thought for actors that says you shouldn't judge your character but, I mean, how else can
you say it: She was dumb. Filled with heart and soul and compassion, but not the sharpest
knife in the drawer.

I think she really did believe that, in the end,
Christopher was going to run away with her. She
was so naïve, so wanted to believe that people had
goodness in them, that they weren't all full of shit.
She couldn't believe Christopher would betray her
like that. And she was frazzled; she had been beat-
en down those last few days. Otherwise, she would
have called the Feds. She would never have gotten
in that car with Silvio.

When they killed her you really got to see
how base these people are. Adriana didn't need to
die. She didn't really give the FBI any fucking information. But they didn't have the patience to figure
that out. They just killed this girl for no reason.
I'd like them to suffer some consequences for that."

MOLL RAT

LET THERE BE NO DOUBT of this one fact: Drea de Matteo loves dogs. When her beloved Great Dane, Cyrus, died several years ago, she had his remains made into a diamond ring. She also has Cyrus's testicles pre-served in a jar, and she refuses to fly her English bulldog, Miss Charlie Rose, to California when she has to go there, opting to make the 3,000 mile drive for the dog's comfort. All of which is to say that it's not any prejudice on de Matteo's part that led to a difficult working relationship with Cosette, Adriana's constant companion. "That dog did not like me," de Matteo says of the combination Maltese and poodle. "She would snap at me and pee on my hands—get up on her front paws, stick her ass in the air and pee. Totally bizarre."

Cosette met her end in Season Four, accidentally sat upon by a drug-addled Christopher. For that scene, prop master Diana Burton fashioned a fake doggie corpse, though she had trou-ble matching one important body part. "Eventually, we wound up using a piece of prosciutto for the tongue," Burton says. The fake tongue, enshrined in a Ziploc baggie, still hangs on the door of *The Sopranos* props closet, a small memo-rial to the show's tiniest whackee.

SILVIO DANTE

"SILVIO IS PROBABLY THE ONLY MEMBER OF THE FAMILY WHO IS HAPPY WHERE HE IS. He's Tony's lifelong friend and the family's *consigliere*. I think he probably had some leadership skills himself, but he realized early on that he didn't like being in the spotlight. He prefers to be behind the curtain.

He's a guy who lives a bit in the past. He doesn't relate to the modern world particularly. He feels a little bit like he missed the boat, wishes he could be part of the thirties or forties or even fifties. All these guys romanticize that past a little bit.

When it comes to the job, Silvio's like ice. Absolute ice. He's going to be very adult, very sophisticated, rarely fly off the handle. He's calm and cool under the most serious life-threatening circumstances. But when it comes to sporting activities or his daughter's soccer games or playing cards, he just completely loses it. That's where he vents his frustrations.

Silvio is sort of the ambassador for the family. He's a diplomat. He's always dealing with the outside world—either to do business or expand it. Paulie Walnuts couldn't survive five minutes outside the world he's in. He'd dry up and die. But not Silvio.

Killing Adriana was a very black-and-white thing. I mean, he's capable of some gray areas. That's part of modern life. He's not a complete barbarian. But certain issues, for him, are just black and white. You're a rat? End of story. No discussion. No emotion. Over. There might be a moment where he thinks, *What a shame. She was such a nice girl.* But at the same time there's going to be self-preservation: What did she say? Am I in danger? Either way, it's a done deal.

Same with Vito. If the situation hadn't been taken out of Silvio's hands, he would have had to recommend that Tony kill Vito. Keep in mind, Silvio does the business, so he knew this guy was a good earner. And maybe he genuinely liked the guy. But, in the end, he knew it was bad for business; that there was going to be less respect. Being gay is probably second only to being a rat. And that will override everything else. In this world, the traditionalist, pragmatic side always wins.

In another life, I think Silvio would have liked to own a sophisticated club. He has a feel for show business. He's a Frank Sinatra, Tony Bennett, Jerry Vale kind of guy. I think he'd like to have the kind of club where there's that kind of entertainment, you know, like the old Copacabana. Instead, he owns the Bada Bing."

WELL-SUITED

BEFORE *THE SOPRANOS*, Steven Van Zandt was, of course, best known as a solo musician, record producer, member of Bruce Springsteen's E Street Band, and a political activist. One thing he hadn't done was act. "I thought, *How am I going to do this?*" he remembers. "I decided I needed to make it work from the outside in. I've got to look like this guy." Among other things, that meant substituting a wig for Van Zandt's trademark headscarves, bulking up in weight ("All of a sudden I was this big guy. I really got into being big"), and above all, sliding on some of the most mind-bending suits this side of a Las Vegas lost-and-found.

"Silvio is special," says costume designer Juliet Polcsa. "Not many people have a maroon striped suit. Not many people have a pink blazer. Not many have a gold sharkskin suit or a green silk sport coat with a black collar. You can't just buy this stuff."

Luckily, Van Zandt's initial research included finding a Newark tailor named Joe Camelia (since relocated to Nutley, New Jersey) who did know how to create such clothing, and more. Camelia's been custom-dressing Silvio ever since.

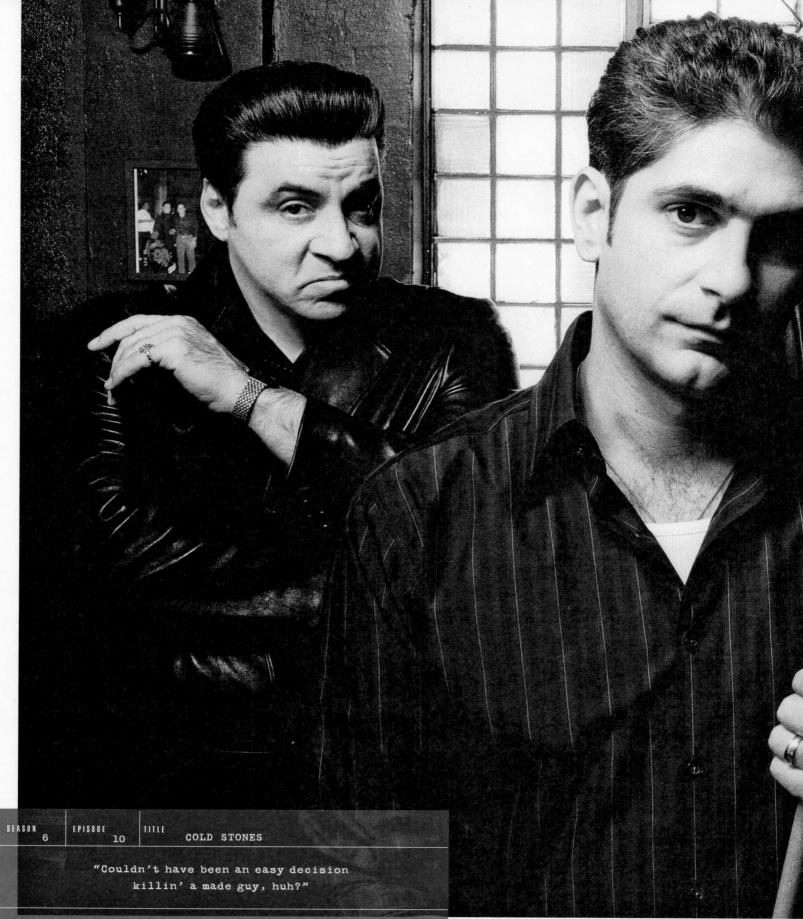

SEASON 6   EPISODE 10   TITLE COLD STONES

"Couldn't have been an easy decision
killin' a made guy, huh?"

ATTRIBUTION   — TONY SOPRANO

PAULIE WALNU

"PAULIE'S SMART. HE'S TOUGH. HE'S GOT A GREAT SENSE OF HUMOR.
HE'S ALSO A KILLER.

Here's how complicated he is: Envision Paulie on one side of the street, beating the
shit out of some guy with a baseball bat. When he's done there, he walks an old lady across
the street. He's been in the mob for thirty-five years—ever since he was driving for Tony
Soprano's father, John. Thirty-five years of living that life and you get cold and stale. You get
a lot of blood on your hands. I mean, how happy can these guys be? But Paulie still hasn't
lost it totally; there is a heart in there. You just have to go deep to get it.

I think Paulie's a realist. He knows he's never going to be the boss. But you'd better not
step on his ground, his piece of territory. In that life, you're always looking to get more.
You've just got to know when to draw the line. A lot of times, Paulie has to bite his lip with
Tony. He wants more, but he has to suck it up because of who he is. Then he takes it out on
other guys. Let me tell you, a lot of people suffer when Tony yells at Paulie.

I don't think he's ever been married. He's been fooling with whores and showgirls
all his life. He wants them to come into the room, shut up, get it done, take the money,
and get out of there. I think the last date Paulie had was in Season Three. I've always
asked David Chase, 'Is he gay?' That's my way of saying I want a dame to squeeze and
hold in front of the camera.

Paulie loves his ma, though. Of course we find out that his ma isn't really his ma.
He was devastated by that because she was a breath of fresh air to this man who has no
air in the life he lives. Eventually he returns to the
only woman who has ever loved him. I thought it
was very touching.

I think about James Cagney every time I do a
scene. You know the way Paulie stands, he's always
got his hands together? That's James Cagney. He's
my idol. Growing up in Brooklyn I knew guys like
that: This one guy, Andy 'The Whip,' I used to
watch a lot. He had a walk, a strut about him. He
took pride in keeping his head up and being cool.
I was enchanted.

Is Paulie evil? Well, he's got a lot of blood on
his hands. He ain't going to heaven, that's for sure.
But I'll tell you something, no matter how crazy
he's been and whatnot, I think a lot of people are
going to miss him when he's gone."

WINGED VICTORY

DON KING. DONALD TRUMP.
Paulie Walnuts. Perhaps
it's best not to dwell on
the similarities between
these three men except for
this: They've all got sensa-
tional, eye-popping impos-
sible-to-picture-on-another-
living-soul hairstyles.

Paulie's trademark silver
"wings" came about almost by
accident. In 1996, Tony Sirico
was cast as an older character
in the HBO movie *Gotti* and let
a little gray creep in on the
sides of his head. "To be honest, I've dyed my hair for so
long, I don't know what its
real color is," he says. He was
still sporting the look when
he auditioned for David Chase,
and the rest is history.

Not that maintaining such
splendor is easy. On days when
he has an early filming call,
Sirico wakes at 3 a.m. and
goes to work in front of the
mirror. By the time he emerges
from his Bay Ridge apartment,
three hours later, the winged
pompadour is in place—not
to be altered, adjusted, or
fussed with by another human
being. "I'm not allowed to
even touch him," says hairstylist Anthony Veader.

"I've been in this busi-
ness a long time. I have my
own ways of doing things,"
explains Sirico. In this
case, the secret is simple:
"A whole can of hairspray.
That's what keeps it standing
up like a man."

TS

BIG PUSSY

BOBBY BACALA

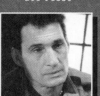

EUGENE PONTECORVO

RALPHIE CIFARETTO

BENNY FAZIO

CHRISTOPHER MOLTISANTI

FURIO GIUNTA

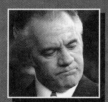

PAULIE WALNUTS

VITO SPATAFORE

SILVIO DANTE

PATSY PARISI

CORRADO "JUNIOR" SOPRANO

JERSEY V

TONY SOPRANO

O F ALL THE THINGS NEW JERSEY IS—ONE OF the original thirteen colonies; the site of decisive Revolutionary War battles and Thomas Edison's laboratory; home to bustling seaports, beautiful beaches, rolling farmland, and the first baseball game (not to mention the most malls in America); in short, a place with plenty to be proud of—it's of course impossible to discuss the state without talking about what it's not, i.e. a certain city across the Hudson River. "New York gets all of the attention and New Jersey is sort of the ugly stepsister," says writer and executive producer Terence Winter. "That kind of informs the attitude of people who live there—and the characters on the show. They're not the Yankees. They're not really even the Mets. There's a kind of underdog defensiveness."

Perhaps nobody is better qualified to comment on this frame of mind than Steven Van Zandt, who, as both the guitarist for Bruce Springsteen's E Street Band and the actor who plays Silvio Dante, is undeniably New Jersey royalty. "I must say that it's interesting to see New Jersey become fashionable twice in my lifetime. I mean, what were the odds of *that*?" Van Zandt says bemusedly. "When Bruce said he wanted to call his first album *Greetings From Asbury Park*,

the record company tried to talk him out of it. You could be from Jersey, but you didn't want to brag about it. It was a joke. The wannabe city."

We can see this mentality at play whenever *The Sopranos*'s relatively small Jersey family interacts with the enormous New York organization run by Carmine Lupertazzi until his death and then taken over by Johnny Sack and Phil Leotardo. Carmine might have dismissed the Sopranos organization as a "glorified crew," but he and the rest of the New Yorkers lick their chops at the prospect of getting a piece of whatever suburban action the Jersey family generates. Tony is none too happy when Sack and his wife, Ginny, move into a north Jersey McMansion, despite Johnny's assurances that he won't "stick his beak" into local affairs. Indeed, on matters large and small—from the neighborhood lawn-care business to the Sopranos's HUD scheme to the Esplanade project to, eventually, the order to kill Tony Blundetto, Tony Soprano's cousin, the New Yorkers cast a long shadow across the river—engendering the kind of frustration and resentment that could be familiar to many New Jerseyites. "New York is like the Death Star and they're a little band of outsiders," Winter says.

JOHNNY "SACK" SACRAMONI

PHIL LEOTARDO

FAT DOM

LITTLE CARMINE LUPERTAZZI

CARMINE LUPERTAZZI

GERRY "THE HAIRDO" TORCIANIO

BUTCH DECONCINI

BOBBY "BACALA" BACCILIERI

"TO BE HONEST, I THINK BOBBY WOULD HAVE BEEN JUST AS HAPPY AS A PLUMBER: work nine-to-five, come home, play with his trains, watch *Jeopardy,* and go to sleep. That would have been a perfectly satisfying life for him. But he was born into the mob. His father was a mobster and he sort of inherited that life.

But I don't think it's glamorous for him. Bobby's not out carousing and fucking around like those other guys. He doesn't really hang around the strip club. He's never had a *goomara.* He's just a nice guy. An innocent. Not the brightest guy, but he knows what he knows, you know?

On the other hand, he must have done some bad stuff to hang around this long. You don't survive in the mob just being some big dumb guy. We've only seen him help break up a union rally, hitting a guy with a baseball bat. And he threatened the union official.

Bobby's father worked for Uncle Junior and, when he moved to Florida, Bobby just inherited the job. He's very loyal to Junior, almost treats him as a father. There was a famous scene where he tells Junior, 'I'm in awe of you.' He was really floundering—just a fat, dumb guy getting abused. You'd catch him crying.

Tony didn't really like Bobby in the beginning. He'd just call him a fat fuck. But later on they started to bond a little. Tony's grateful that he's taking care of Junior, and Bobby becomes kind of a conduit between them. And Bobby's gotten more assertive, earned a little more respect. He's not as scared of Tony anymore.

I think Bobby was happy before his wife was killed in a car accident. But then he got manipulated by Janice. He'd lost his wife. He was completely broken up. So, he was kind of blind that she's such a psycho. I think Janice is one of the most despicable characters in TV history. She's a murderer, a manipulator. She's horrible to those kids. And yet, she did fight that soccer mom when she thought her daughter was being abused. She will defend her family and Bobby, if not for them then for herself: 'You're not going to fuck with my guy. I can abuse him but you can't.'

And you know what? Maybe Bobby isn't so stupid after all. He's moved up through the ranks. He's moved into a bigger house. Maybe marrying the boss's sister wasn't the worst idea in the world. She may be a little crazy, but now he's Tony Soprano's brother-in-law. He's got a seat at the Sunday table."

"COME HEAVY OR NOT AT ALL"

WHEN STEVE SCHIRRIPA got the first pages of script for his new role as Bobby Bacala, he couldn't help but notice a certain theme to the dialogue. "There were all these fat jokes from Tony: 'You're a calzone with legs.' 'I seriously suggest you start eating salads.' 'Fat fuck' this, 'fat fuck' that. I thought, *I know I'm fat, but I'm not that much fatter than Tony.* It just didn't make sense," he remembers.

Schirripa seriously considered the possibility that the show had hired the wrong actor until he showed up for his costume fitting and was informed that he'd be wearing a prosthetic fat suit. "David [Chase] wanted this character to be really big, a big slovenly guy," says Juliet Polcsa. "So we had to give poor Steve another fifty pounds."

"I felt like the Michelin man," Schirripa says. The indignity ended at the beginning of Season Four when Schirripa ran into Chase at Silvercup Studios. Chase looked him up and down and informed Polcsa that the fat suit would no longer be needed. "I guess he figured I was fat enough on my own now," says Schirripa.

CRIME MAKEUP

ADD THIS TO THE LIST OF THINGS YOU SHOULD Avoid If You Are a *Sopranos* Character at Risk: Don't take a call from Steve Kelley.

Kelley and his wife, Kymbra Callaghan Kelley, share duties as makeup artists on *The Sopranos*, and making people look beautiful is only half the job. Along with such makeup-trailer fixtures as mascara, blush, and lipstick, *The Sopranos* trailer contains closets filled with fake blood and bins of prosthetic gunshot wounds.

"They tell us someone's going to be shot and we ask, 'Head shot or body shot? What size bullets? You want entrance wounds or exit wounds?'" Steve says.

There are reference books filled with pictures of bodies violated in unimaginable ways and others showing corpses in various states of decomposition. "That one looks like lasagna," Kymbra says appreciatively, looking at a mottled arm of a body fished out of a lake after an untold number of weeks. Then she returns to applying blush to Edie Falco, who has barely blinked.

But the most gruesome tasks fall to Steve, who is in charge of creating large-scale prosthetics—like Tony's shot-up stomach or

Ralph Cifaretto's head and hands. Usually, being called in to have your body measured for such a prosthetic means bad news for the actor. "The actors will come in here and look around like, 'What have you heard? Am I going?'" says Steve.

Sometimes, the work is hazardous in and of itself. During Season Six, Steve was told to make prosthetic heads for Fat Dom, the New York soldier killed in the back of Satriale's Pork Store by Silvio and Carlo. He was up late in his New Jersey studio making six different versions, including copies to be seen in the Satriale's freezer and others to be kicked down a storm drain in south Jersey. The next morning, exhausted, he set out for work and got

VARIETIES OF BLOOD TO BE FOUND IN *THE SOPRANOS* MAKEUP CABINET: A PARTIAL LIST

LIGHT BLOOD • DARK BLOOD • CLOTTED BLOOD • RUNNING BLOOD • DRIED BLOOD • DARK BLOODY GOOP • LIGHT BLOODY GOOP • EYE BLOOD • MOUTH BLOOD • DARK MOUTH BLOOD SYRUP • LIGHT MOUTH BLOOD SYRUP • BLOODY BLOOD JELLY • REAL BLOODY BLOOD

into a fender bender on the George Washington Bridge. In the backseat, wrapped in black plastic garbage bags, were the six heads. In the collision, two came free and were rolling around on the floor. "The policewoman walks over to check out the damage in the car and I see her look in the backseat and put her hand on her gun," Kelley remembers.

In a remarkable sign of loyalty to the show—or the mortal fear instilled by its producers—Kelley's first thought was to not give any plot secrets away. "I had to talk really fast, but really calm," he says. "I just said that I worked for a production around town and slowly her hand left the gun. But, yeah, *The Sopranos* almost got me shot."

The makeup department creates wigs for Tony Sirico's stunt man and Steven Van Zandt, as well as creating believable pools of blood at various crime scenes.

THE LEGENDARY BACK ROOMS OF

SATRIALE'S
PORK STORE

In the mob, the role of the social club is paramount. A made man is nothing without his hangout. "It's like a presidential library," says Bob Shaw. "Everybody gets one."

THE KITCHEN/DINING ROOM

On the walls are Italian travel posters, a strange wooden flounder and, of course, a collection of taxidermy worthy of Teddy Roosevelt. "It's their anchor in the old world," says Shaw.

THE MEAT CUTTER

The meat cutter just outside of the back office has been useful in disposing of bodies.

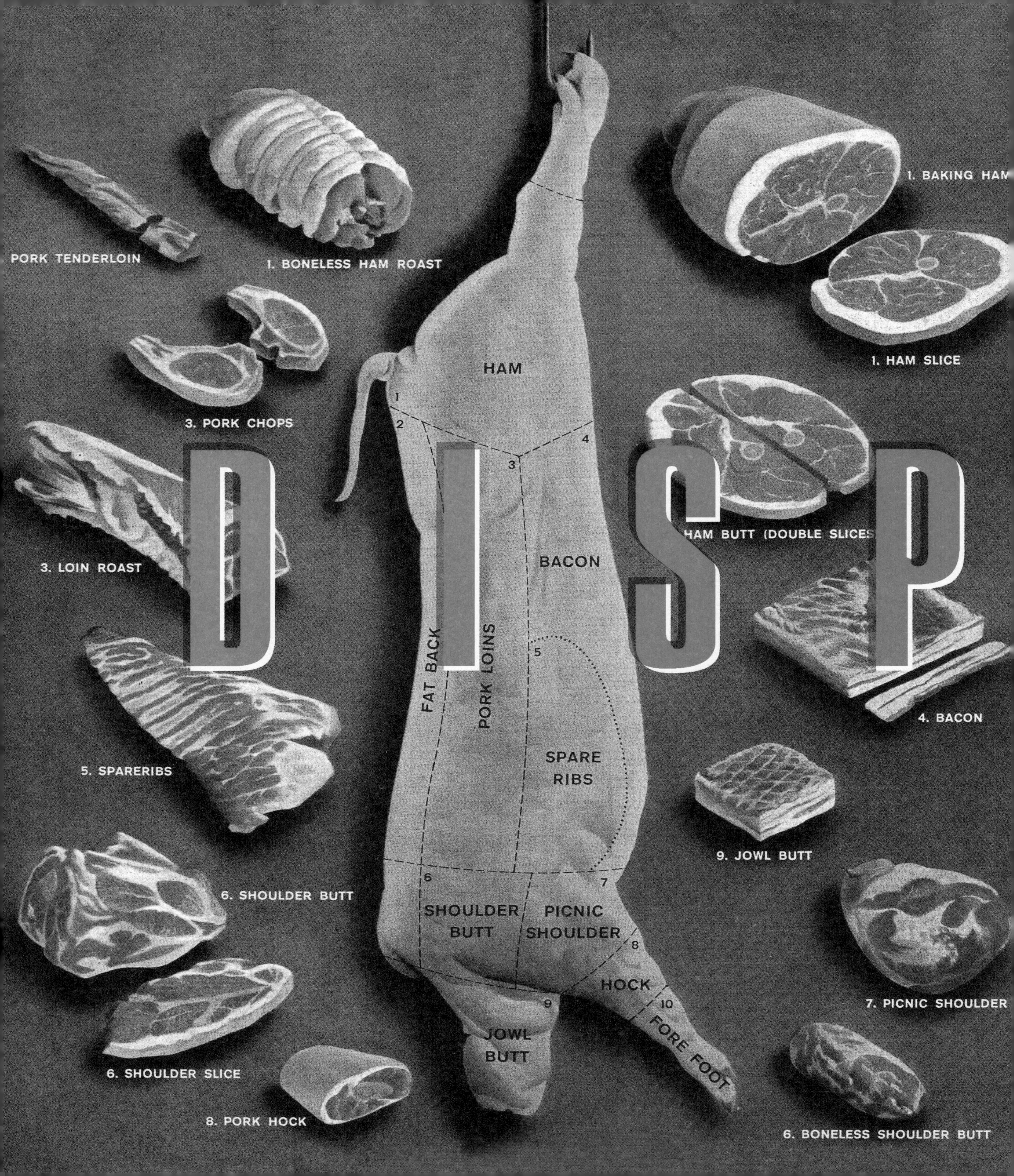

PORK TENDERLOIN

1. BONELESS HAM ROAST

1. BAKING HAM

1. HAM SLICE

3. PORK CHOPS

3. LOIN ROAST

HAM

HAM BUTT (DOUBLE SLICES)

BACON

FAT BACK

PORK LOINS

5. SPARERIBS

4. BACON

SPARE RIBS

9. JOWL BUTT

6. SHOULDER BUTT

SHOULDER BUTT

PICNIC SHOULDER

7. PICNIC SHOULDER

HOCK

6. SHOULDER SLICE

JOWL BUTT

FORE FOOT

8. PORK HOCK

6. BONELESS SHOULDER BUTT

O S A L

"IT'S GONNA BE A WHILE BEFORE I EAT ANYTHING FROM SATRIALE'S."

—CHRISTOPHER MOLTISANTI

CHAPTER 7

"THIS THIN

A5:8 25:B

SOPRANOS

A. COULTER

P. ABRAHAM

G OF OURS"

CREATING *THE SOPRANOS* UNIVERSE

ANY WAY YOU SLICE IT,

THE SOPRANOS IS A MASSIVE ENTERPRISE.

THERE ARE COSTUME DESIGNERS AND MAKEUP DESIGNERS; LOCATION SCOUTS AND SET BUILDERS; SOUND ENGINEERS, CAMERA OPERATORS, LIGHTING TECHNICIANS, PROP MASTERS, SCENIC PAINTERS, AND SCRIPT SUPERVISORS.

There are first assistant directors, second assistant directors, and second-second assistant directors. There are gaffers and best boys; lamp operators and accountants; security guards and truck drivers and parking coordinators and caterers and medics and something called the "Base Camp Genny Operator." There are many, many production assistants.

Every one of these people, and many more—the equivalent workforce of a small city—labor in service of one thing: telling *The Sopranos* story. Everything begins with the story and the story begins in the head of one man, David Chase.

"ALWAYS WITH THE SCENARIOS."
—SILVIO DANTE

AFTER EACH SERIES HIATUS, CHASE returns to work with a series of 11x17" pieces of graph paper taped together and covered in neat type. Unfurled, the resulting document is a map of the coming season. Running from left to right and stacked neatly atop one another are each character's storylines, divided into thirteen episodes. By scanning down the "Episode Four" column, say, you could see what Tony will be doing at that point in the season; below him, Carmela; then Meadow, A.J., Paulie, and so forth. "Some characters have more than one storyline. Tony may have three or four," says Chase. "His story with Carmela, his story with his crew, his story with Phil Leotardo. If you took an episode like Johnny Sack's daughter's wedding, in Season Six, you'd see Tony trying to recover from being shot, Tony dealing with Johnny Sack, and then Johnny's own storyline, Vito's storyline, and so on."

The ever-growing profusion of stories may be natural on a show that has run for almost one hundred hours, but it also springs from a built-in problem *The Sopranos* faced following its first season. "You have to understand that most scripts don't get made into pilots. Most pilots don't get made into shows, and most shows don't run for more than five episodes. So, in writing the first season, all I thought about—narratively—was getting through the season," Chase says. The problem was that the first season constituted a nearly self-contained story and there was no clear way forward once Chase had to formulate Season Two.

"Basically there were three actors in the drama: A man, his mother, and his uncle. But then Livia had a stroke, and Uncle Junior tried to kill Tony, so it turned out that neither of them would be interacting with the main character much anymore. We had lost two of our main pistons. So we had to bring in Richie Aprile. We had Tony's sister come back. And, immediately, the stories began becoming more and more complicated."

"YOU KNOW WHO HAD AN ARC? NOAH."
—BIG PUSSY BONPENSIERI

CHASE'S OUTLINE IS BROUGHT INTO THE writers' room, a spacious conference room at Silvercup Studios with dramatic views of the Manhattan skyline and the Queensborough Bridge. In the center of the room is a long table covered in pens and legal pads; there are also fidgety-writer-friendly packets of gum, mints, and toothpicks. On the walls are seven white dry-erase boards that are eventually covered in scribbled themes and plot points, half-formed jokes, and fragments of dialogue. A framed photo of Fellini looks on from one wall. "It's pretty much like every other writers' room I've ever been in," says writer and executive producer Matthew Weiner, a veteran of such shows as *Becker* and *Andy Richter Controls the Universe*. After a week or two of sitting around the table, avoiding working, wrestling with the season's overall themes and character arcs, the writers will begin to think in terms of individual episodes. "We ask ourselves, 'Okay, what stories are we *really* going to tell? What is this week's movie going to be about?'" Chase says, explaining the difference between the narrative business each episode is required to dispense with and its actual plot. "Maybe the outline says, 'Tony and Phil argue about construction kickbacks.' But then we get in the room and say, 'We can do that with two lines of dialogue. Let's make the story about—to take an example—the Italian neighborhood church feast. It can all be about the feast with two lines about construction kickbacks. So it's a small movie about a feast, or a small movie about being lost in the wilderness."

Sometimes, an episode will offer a self-contained story tucked into the overall plot. These are often inspired by questions that come up around the writers' table: What would happen if a made man hit the lottery and tried to retire? (Answer: Nothing very

good, as Eugene Pontecorvo learned at the start of Season Six.) Other times, individual episodes will explore a specific theme. "*The Sopranos* is probably the first show in the history of television to do an hour-long episode on the subject of boredom," says Weiner of Season Six's "The Ride," in which Tony rediscovers his outlaw spark by lifting a few cases of wine from an idling truck and Christopher once again falls off the wagon. Still other times, the route to a major plot point can take unexpected shape. The outline for Season Five specified that Tony and Carmela start getting back together by the end of the eleventh episode. It was only in the writers' room that the path to reconciliation emerged as the extended "Test Dream" Tony has while checked into the Plaza Hotel.

As each episode takes shape, Chase and the writers begin to map out the hour on the white-boards—breaking the action down into a series of scenes or "beats": CARMELA AND A.J. ARGUE, one might read. Or, for that matter, TONY KILLS RALPHIE. Most beats will be attached to important bits of dialogue. After being shot by Uncle Junior, "Tony was going to be struggling with the feeling that he'd been throwing away his time and energy on things that weren't important," says Chase. Up on the board went the line "EVERY DAY IS A GIFT."

Once an episode is roughly blocked out on the board, a writers' assistant types the list of scenes. He then prints the page and cuts it into strips, one per beat, which can be physically arranged and rearranged on the conference table until the story is flowing just right. At that point, the writer who has been assigned to take the lead on that episode takes the finished outline and writes a first draft. By the time Chase has made his notes and the other writers theirs, and the script has gone through the countless adjustments, tweaks, and overhauls necessitated by the realities of filming and production, it's not unusual to be on draft number twelve or higher. And then, of course, everything can still change in the editing room. In fact, it does.

"OH, THE LANGUAGE ON YOU! YOU BLOW YOUR FATHER WITH THAT MOUTH?"
—TONY SOPRANO

IT'S NO SECRET THAT CHASE HAS FIRED writers over the years, whitling his staff down to a small group who, he says, "are always firing on all cylinders."

"David has always said that he's not running a writing class," says Terence Winter, who joined the show as a writer and producer during Season Two. "Either you get the show or you don't." Says Chase, "The people who have written the show best have an astonishing ability to do hairpin turns. They can go from sadness, to very strong threat behavior, to goofball humor, all in a few seconds."

At *The Sopranos* the script has always been king (ad-libbing has never been a part of the show), which means that everything that needs to be onscreen needs first to be in the script—often at a surprising level of specificity.

"David expects you to commit to details as much as he does. Nothing's left to chance," says Michael Imperioli who, in addition to playing Christopher Moltisanti, has written five episodes. "It's never 'Carmela goes to the door and the delivery boy gives her the birthday cake.' It's 'Carmela goes to the door and the delivery boy is a nineteen-year-old Brazilian guy wearing an Artuso's Pastry Shop baseball cap—and he has a lisp.' Or, they'll go to the hospital and the emergency room doctor is 'a Sikh with a turban but no accent.' And then when they cast it, they really go find that nineteen-year-old Brazilian or that Sikh."

Writing for *The Sopranos* has other special requirements. It helps, for instance, to have a finely tuned sense and appreciation of how men curse. It's probably a good sign if you can actually make yourself cringe at the crudeness of what you yourself have just written. "Whatever my next job is, I'm reasonably sure that I won't be able to have one character tell another to 'Stop being cunty,'" Winter says with no small measure of satisfaction.

Another distinctive feature of *The Sopranos* language is Chase's love for old-fashioned Italian-American slang. When Fat Dom was stabbed at Satriale's Pork Store, Chase wrote a line for Silvio: "We've got to clean this up. Go get some *biangalin'*."

"Everybody was scratching their heads, wondering what *biangalin'* was," says Andrew Schneider, who joined the writing staff with his wife, Diane Frolov, for the show's last two seasons. "It turned out to be this very specific New Jersey Italian word for 'bleach,'" says Schneider. "The great thing is that David doesn't care if most of the audience has no idea what Silvio said. He's happy if three percent will be delighted by hearing that word."

David Chase's preliminary story ideas for Season Two.

> **"DAVID EXPECTS YOU TO COMMIT TO DETAILS AS MUCH AS HE DOES. NOTHING'S LEFT TO CHANCE," SAYS MICHAEL IMPERIOLI.**

1.) AJ in NY
2.) Melfi raped
3.) Carmela/priest
4.) Carmela and Frank
5.) Tony/Carmela vacation
6.) Meadow's gangsta boyfriend
7.) Livia/Tony scene
8.) Another Flashback
9.) Fever dream
10.) Livia takes Prozac and becomes great gal
11.) AJ absentee lottery

17.) Richie's ballroom dancing son
18.) Richie's sexual confusion
19.) The Columbus hit back
20.) Bing Girl story
21.) Paulie obsession with spy technology
22.) Provincial differences
23.) Janice rips up the walls
24.) Janice as mafia princess
25.) Janice wants Harpo
26.) State of Washington investigators
27.) Melfi's son and ... Bard hijinks
28.) Webistics pays off
29.) Telephone cards and Pakis
30.) Carmela/Angie fight — divided by ...

And then there are the malapropisms—those words and expressions that characters alter, confuse, or downright mangle, often in an attempt to sound smarter than they are. Malaprops litter *The Sopranos* scripts in instances both small (Christopher is fond of using "infer" when he means "imply"), large (Little Carmine convenes a sit-down by saying, "Certain incidents have recently expired"), and inadvertently brilliant (Little Carmine characterizes his rift with Johnny Sack as a "stagmire"). Often, Tony will pick up an expression at Dr. Melfi's office and later misuse it; "Cap D'Antibes" became "Captain Teebs"; *"amour fou"* mutated into "our mofo."

"There have been times when we've taken out a funny line because somebody in the writers' room says, 'Tony would know that word. He wouldn't get it wrong,'" says Winter. "You don't want to be throwing in jokes for the sake of jokes."

And while the character's linguistic crimes are often played for laughs, they also illuminate something more universal, says Chase. "It's what you see around you all the time: People trying to bullshit their way through conversations without knowing what they're talking about," he says. "You see it in Harvard graduates and you see it in high school dropouts. I do it myself all the time. Like right now."

Above all, what defines *The Sopranos* writing is a commitment to giving each character his or her own unique voice. Even among the wise guys, it is easy to distinguish, say, Silvio's baroque wisdoms ("Sadness accrues") from Paulie's rougher edges (on Big Pussy: "I loved that cocksucker like a brother, and he fucked me in the ass").

"All the writers on this show appreciate characters. Not just collections of traits and TV foibles that can be trotted out interchangeably, but real, unpredictable entities who can go anyplace and say anything," says Chase. "I think that came from growing up with my extended family. Each aunt or uncle was a different character: Aunt Gemma was different from Aunt Livia; Uncle Augie

> # "ALL THE WRITERS ON THIS SHOW APPRECIATE CHARACTERS....REAL, UNPREDICTABLE ENTITIES WHO CAN GO ANYPLACE AND SAY ANYTHING."

FIVE GREAT MALAPROPISMS
(An Arbitrary List)

1.	TONY SOPRANO: Meadow still here? CARMELA SOPRANO: Jackie Jr. took her to the city to see *Aida*. TONY SOPRANO: *I-eat-her?!*
2.	TONY SOPRANO: The Hitlers, the Paul Pots. Those are the evil fucks that deserve to die.
3.	CHRISTOPHER MOLTISANTI (*on unrest in the New York Family*): Why not? Create a little dysentery in the ranks.
4.	CARMINE LUPERTAZZI (*on Tony's being in therapy*): Don't worry—there's no stigmata.
5.	TONY SOPRANO: When she stares at ya it's like, uh, like a Spanish princess in one a those paintin's, ya know, a Goyim.

was different from Uncle Carmine. They *spoke* differently. And that's what I always thought was the job of literature. You read *Death of a Salesman* and Biff doesn't sound like Happy, who doesn't sound like Willy Loman."

Often, on *The Sopranos*, that has meant writing for unsophisticated, not overly educated human beings, confused beings, inarticulate beings—at the very least for people who (with the notable exception of Tony and Dr. Melfi during their therapy scenes) rarely say what they really mean. "These people aren't necessarily articulate, but they do have enormous insight," says Chase. "They intuitively know how to flip every conversation to their advantage: 'How am I going to get what's mine?' Our writers understand that, and they understand that this is a culture of breaking balls—sometimes it's a joke, but sometimes it's not."

One would think that this would be, at times, a challenging bit of ventriloquism—like a great dancer trying to fake clumsiness—but Chase says that it comes easily. "Everybody who writes for the show will tell you that, for some reason, when you put these characters in the right situation, they just go by themselves," he says. "Once they start to talk, you can just keep writing and writing and writing."

"MORE IS LOST BY INDECISION THAN WRONG DECISION."

—TONY SOPRANO

AS EACH EPISODE NEARS THE START OF filming, *The Sopranos*'s key creative players convene at what is known as a tone meeting. As with much of television, a medium driven by writers to a much larger extent than film, directors change from episode to episode, though a handful—chief among them Tim Van Patten, Allen Coulter, Alan Taylor, and the late John Patterson—have returned for multiple installments.

"Timmy, Alan, and these other guys, they understand what we do," says executive producer Ilene Landress. "Our thing with directors is that we don't need people to come in and reinvent the show with self-conscious camera work or gimmicks. In general, self-consciousness is something we fight against."

If an episode is going to involve any kind of stylistic departure from the classic style of *The Sopranos*—say, the hallucinatory drug montage of "The Ride," it will be one of the things discussed at the tone meeting. At the meeting are Chase and Landress, Winter, Weiner, Schneider or Frolov, one of the show's two directors of photography (who alternate episodes), the assistant director, UPM/co-executive producer Henry Bronchtein, and, on the phone from Los Angeles, the post-production team. Page by page, the director presents his vision of the script to the group, asking questions and making adjustments.

"Sometimes you're in there and you feel all these eyes on you and you really don't know what to say about a certain scene," says Steve Buscemi, who has directed four episodes. "I just say, 'Well, I think this means this.' And either David agrees or he explains a different way to look at it."

"Often if somebody asks a question like, 'What does this dream sequence mean?' David won't answer," says producer Gianna Smart. "Or he'll turn the question back to you. It's almost like he's asking us all to make up our own minds, which is extraordinary. Usually in TV they lead you by the nose, but David really wants you to think."

James Gandolfini and Tony Sirico shoot a scene from the Season Two episode, "From Here to Eternity."

The next stop for the new script is the production meeting, and this is where the episode picks up speed. The meeting gathers the heads of all the departments relevant to the formidable task of putting what's on paper on the screen—costumes, props, makeup, locations, scenic, sets, etc. The production meeting is father to a thousand lists, as each department breaks the script down into relevant components. Meanwhile the director of photography assigned to that episode—Alik Sakharov and Phil Abraham alternate DP duties from episode to episode—will be breaking down the script into a shot list. According to Sakharov, who has been with the show since filming the pilot episode, this is both a practical exercise—figuring out the logistics of capturing each scene on film while sticking to a budget and schedule—and something more abstract. "The way David Chase writes, and all the show's writers write, is very visual," says Sakharov. "As you read, the picture unfolds in your head. And that allows you to set up an image that, hopefully, reflects the emotional condition of the actors."

Above: Director of photography Alik Sakharov and director Tim Van Patten. Below: James Gandolfini behind the camera.

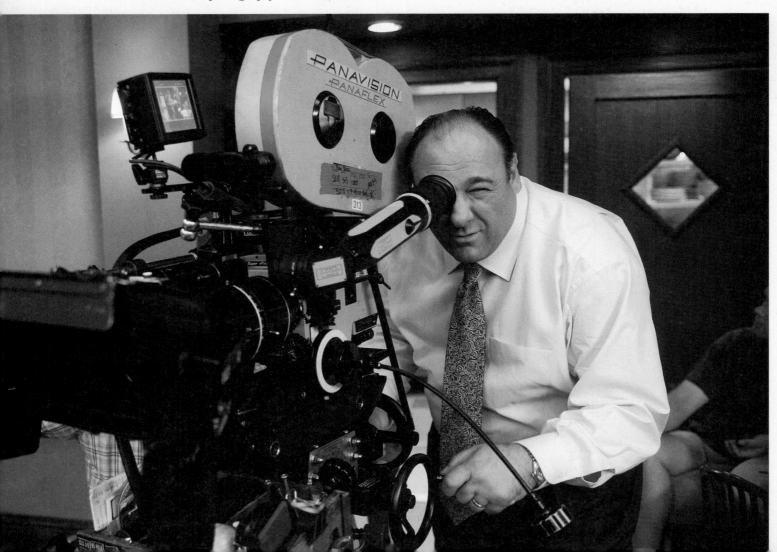

The foundation for that subtle interaction between light and character was already evident in the pilot. When, for instance, Tony, Christopher, and Hesh met to discuss business in the VIP area of the Bada Bing, they were practically consumed by shadows. Likewise, Christopher psyched himself up for his first murder by doing Tai Chi at the pork store. "There are a million ways to shoot a pork store," Sakharov says. "It was nighttime. There was a clandestine meeting going on. I thought there should be an air of mystery. So, I went with a very dark, almost *chiaroscuro* effect."

Early on in the life of the show, Sakharov and Abraham's camera work was slightly more giddy, filled with odd angles and bright colors, but it soon became apparent that such self-conscious strokes were unnecessary. "The story was so strong that you didn't have to emphasize it with expressive camera work," Sakharov says. "The idea is to just give a few strokes and let the viewers come along for the ride."

"I REALLY CAN'T BE SEEN IN A PLACE LIKE THIS ANYMORE."
—CHRISTOPHER MOLTISANTI

ONE OF THE FIRST DECISIONS TO BE MADE INVOLVES where things will be filmed—on location or on sets constructed at Silvercup Studios in Queens. Though filming in New Jersey is one of the signature features of *The Sopranos* production (some 66 percent of shooting days takes place on location), several recurring sets are at Silvercup: the Soprano's house, the back rooms of the Bada Bing and Satriale's Pork Store, Dr. Melfi's office, and the dining room and kitchen of Nuovo Vesuvio's. When Tony pulls up to his driveway or barbecues in his backyard, the scene is shot at an actual house in North Caldwell; once he steps inside, though, he's on set in Queens. The famous pool, glimpsed through the kitchen windows, is printed on an enormous, backlit curtain (the translight) that looks like it belongs on a giant shower.

THE WAY DAVID CHASE WRITES, AND ALL THE SHOW'S WRITERS WRITE, IS VERY VISUAL...AS YOU READ, THE PICTURE UNFOLDS IN YOUR HEAD.

Deciding which sets to build and when to shoot on location is a tricky business, especially since not even Landress, who is in charge of such decisions, knows what developments will emerge in coming scripts. At the beginning of Season Six, for instance, when Tony was convalescing from a shot in the stomach, an enormous hospital set was built at Silvercup. This made sense, since Tony wasn't supposed to be released until Episode Five. As it happened, the writers decided to move the story along more quickly, throwing one bum script in the garbage, and their patient went home early. "It's a calculated risk," says Landress, with a shrug. "We go where the story takes us."

Sometimes "the story" works in mysterious ways—like raising the dead. In Season Four, Tony learned that his ex-*goomara* Gloria Trillo (played by Annabella Sciorra) had committed suicide. Feeling safe, Landress and production designer Bob Shaw dismantled the set of Gloria's living room and incorporated it into a new apartment set for Furio Giunta. A few episodes later, Gloria and, more importantly, her house, reappeared in a dream sequence. "We actually had to put it back

The Sopranos is filmed at Silvercup Studios in Queens, New York.

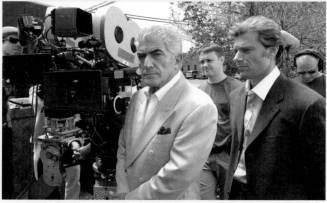

David Chase, Michael Imperioli (Christopher Moltisanti),
and Frank Vincent (Phil Leotardo) on set.

together from bits and pieces," Shaw laughs. "Luckily, it was a dream, so it was okay if things were slightly off. After that, I was afraid to throw anything away."

At times, the art department will be challenged to reproduce a set from the real world. The New York Family's social club, for instance, was shot for several seasons in a real bar, named Mare Chiaro, in Manhattan's Little Italy. That was until a new owner installed an array of flat-screen TVs, fundamentally altering the old-school look of the place. A perfect simulacrum of Mare Chiaro now resides at Silvercup.

Likewise, when Tony shot his cousin Tony Blundetto at the end of Season Five, the scene was originally filmed on the porch of a house in upstate New York. When Chase saw the footage, however, he was unhappy. "I think he wanted me to be looking more directly at the camera," says Steve Buscemi, who played Blundetto. So, the entire porch—or at least that portion of it visible in a tight shot—was reproduced indoors.

As with many elements of filmmaking, the best sign of a good art department may be when you don't notice their work at all. In Season Six, Shaw and his crew were called upon to create a corporate coffee franchise, from scratch, in a Newark storefront. They designed a logo and uniforms, fabricated cups with cardboard sleeves, created little tins of overpriced after-coffee mints, and even made CDs to be sold by the counter—all so that you never doubted for a moment that it was a real store when Patsy Parisi came to shake the place down.

Shaw says that it all comes down to what could be the credo of the entire *The Sopranos* crew: "We go to extraordinary lengths to bring you the ordinary."

> "I DON'T HAVE ANTIQUES.
> MY HOUSE IS TRADITIONAL."
> —CARMELA SOPRANO

ANOTHER PERSON COMBING THROUGH THE script and making lists is prop master Diana Burton, who is responsible for anything an actor picks up, carries, or handles on screen. (Anything worn falls under the aegis of the costume department; anything that just sits on set, like Dr. Melfi's statues, belongs to set dressing; if Tony were to pick *up* the statue, it would suddenly become a prop.)

Making sure that every cash-stuffed envelope, every tray of ziti and glass of whisky, every baseball bat and crowbar, and every wire taped to every rat's body is in the right place at the right time—usually in at least duplicate or triplicate—is no small job. Burton is also in charge of guns, which she rents from a firearms company in Manhattan. "These guys don't hold onto their guns for long," she says, explaining why the production doesn't keep weapons on hand. "They shoot them and then dump them."

The props umbrella also covers vehicles, from Tony's boat and Christopher's Maserati to Carmela's Porsche and A.J.'s yellow Nissan Xterra. This being America, the choice of car that Burton and the writers bestow on a character goes a long way toward defining who they are.

"Vehicles tell a lot about people," Burton says. "Paulie drives a Cadillac CTS because he's a little old-fashioned. Silvio has a black Denali SUV. He certainly can't have an Escalade, because Tony has an Escalade. So, he has a similar car, just not quite as nice. Carmela just traded in her Mercedes wagon for the Cayenne because it's flashier. Status is important to these people."

Then there are props that are more, well, unique—like a wooden bust of Ronald Reagan, with grotesquely enlarged lips, that tips Tony off to a rat when he's visiting colleges with Meadow; or Ralph Cifaretto's detached head and hands; or the talking tilefish that appears in Tony's dream and speaks in Big Pussy's voice.

Props also include animals of the live, nonverbal kind. These have provided some of the more taxing moments in Burton's three years on *The Sopranos*. In Season Four, she was responsible for procuring an equine actor to play Tony's horse, Pie-O-My. Shortly before one of the horse's more complicated scenes, the chosen animal tore its leg on some barbed wire, necessitating a stand-in. "The scene was in the stable. You can hear rain beating on the tin roof. The horse is lying down and Tony comes in, sits on a stool, and lights a cigar. Then, a couple of seconds later, while he's petting the horse, this goat comes in the door, so it creates this kind of trinity. Nice scene, but we had this new high-strung horse that didn't want to lie down, a burning cigar, the rain drowning everything out, and this goat," Burton remembers, imparting a bit of wisdom they should probably teach every student in film school: "Believe me, it's hard to get a goat to do much of anything."

ONE OF THE MORE FUN AREAS TO PASS through at Silvercup Studios is *The Sopranos* scenic department, which, roughly speaking, is in charge of all design elements that involve paint. One day the department will be hard at work creating four versions of, say, a ceramic sculpture for one character to throw at another—two out of plastic, to be thrown, two more out of breakaway plaster to be seen shattering on the floor. The next day, the same space will be turned over to expertly recreating the weathered wood of a farmhouse door, or piles of asbestos, or hospital emergency room signs, or an entire stone fireplace. Scenic is also responsible for such classic artifacts as

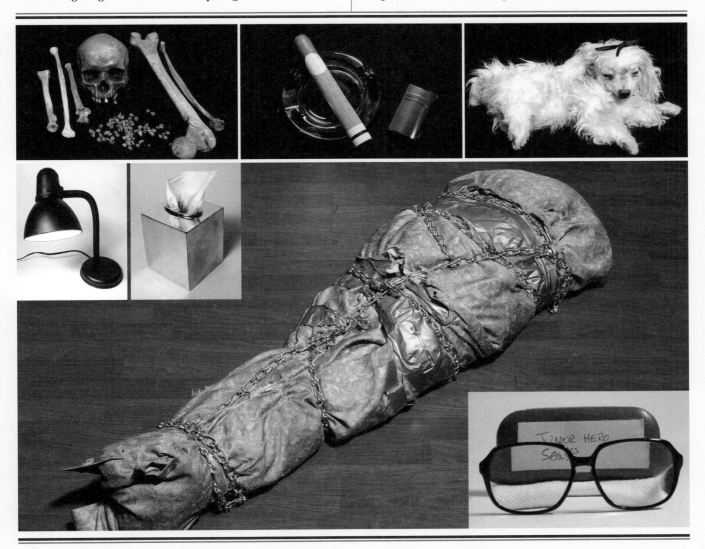

Dead dogs, cigars, eyeglasses, and leftover body parts are some of the props that can be found on set.

the portrait of Tony as a Revolutionary War general, commissioned by Paulie Walnuts, and the creative vandalism perpetrated by Little Paulie on a restaurant owned by Carmine Lupertazzi. "For three weeks, I was sending David sketches of erect penises," says scenic chief Anne Haywood. (It was supposed to look like a Venetian gondola). "He kept sending them back saying, 'A little curvier' or 'Not so long.' Finally I said, 'David, I bet I've seen more of these than you.'"

"WHAT'S NEXT? YOU GET CLIPPED FOR WEARIN' THE WRONG SHOES?"

—ALBERT BARESE

IN A GRAND, PERIOD DRAMA—SOMETHING BY Dickens or Austen, perhaps—the job of the costume designer is to illuminate the full social spectrum of a particular time and place through clothing. That the world happens to be New Jersey, the time happens to be the present, and that some of the clothes happen to be available at Mandee or Caché, doesn't make this any less true of *The Sopranos*.

"From the moment the audience sees a character, even before he or she speaks, you should know a lot about them—what kind of person they are, what class, what they find important," says costume designer Juliet Polcsa, who has been with *The Sopranos* since Season One. "All that comes through the clothes."

As the boss, for instance, Tony dresses more sedately than some of his crew. "He has a certain elegance that, say, Paulie doesn't have," says Polcsa. "Although he also loves those print shirts and there's nothing very elegant about them. Jim [Gandolfini] puts those shirts on and he says he immediately feels like the character." ("Those are the sad clown shirts," Gandolfini says. "Laughing on the outside, crying on the inside.")

Carmela, too, has her own style, Polcsa says: colorful, lots of embellishment, revealing but not trashy. "There's a color, it's like the coral color of cooked shrimp, that we hit upon early in the show. I see that color and it's Carmela." The show's other women, meanwhile, are dressed almost to intentionally contrast with Mrs. Soprano: Dr. Melfi sticks to the more sedate earth tones appropriate for a professional woman (though she's not above showing a little leg); Adriana is . . . well, Adriana—she of the Spandex hotpants and leopard-print tank tops. "Occasionally I would think we were crossing the line into parody but then I'd be shopping at a mall in Jersey and say, 'Nope. We're okay.'"

In the costume department's space at Silvercup, there are neatly catalogued rows of clothes for each character, plus racks of police, doctor, and other assorted uniforms, stripper outfits ("We have a full line of G-strings and see-through pumps," Polcsa says) and a section labeled "Goombah Sets." When an outfit is chosen, it is labeled with a computer-generated tag that lists exactly where and when it appeared on camera. Then, after shooting, it is retired to a far section of the costume department, up near the rafters, nicknamed "Green Grove" after *The Sopranos*'s fictional nursing home. (Retired clothes are said to be "green-groved.")

As with every aspect of *The Sopranos*, absolutely nothing is left to chance. When Tony waded into his swimming pool in his bathrobe to meet the ducks in the very first episode, the robe spread out across the water thanks to corks sewn into its hem. When the script called for a character to pee in his pants, Polcsa and her crew worked for several days determining exactly which fabrics would best highlight the spreading stain.

Polcsa does allow some cast members to contribute their own costume elements. Silvio's astonishing suits, for example, come from a tailor that Steven Van Zandt found in Newark shortly after

The scenic and costume departments play a pivotal role in creating the realistic world of *The Sopranos*.

being cast. And then there are Paulie Walnuts's signature white Vikings, which Tony Sirico wore to his first audition. "They're sort of slippers, sort of loafers, but they're not really either," Polcsa says, with just the slightest wince. "They are *all* Paulie."

> ## "LATELY, I'M GETTING THE FEELING THAT I CAME IN AT THE END."
> —TONY SOPRANO

FOR ALL THE PREPARATION AND WORK THAT goes into writing, designing, and producing each episode of *The Sopranos*, the end of shooting is hardly the end of the story. First, the post-production team in Los Angeles, led by producers Martin Bruestle and Gianna Smart, along with longtime editors Bill Stitch and Sydney Wolinsky, piece together the episode as scripted. "We're not there to rearrange anything," says Smart. "We follow the script."

Nevertheless, this initial edit is a creative process as the editors comb through dozens of takes and coverages, searching for the best way to tell the story. "I know for a fact that I have been horrible, just plain *bad* at times, and that the editors have saved me," says James Gandolfini.

The post-production team is responsible for mixing sound, correcting color, and looping dialogue—all, they hope, invisible processes that nonetheless have a subtle effect on the story. They are also responsible for digital effects. There are times that, instead of using makeup to create a gunshot, it makes more sense to digitally insert blood, gore, and smoke. Often, effects are necessary to preserve continuity: digital artists added clouds of freezing breath to the van scenes from "Pine Barrens," actually shot on a soundstage at Silvercup. One reshot scene

Quintessential outfits for Adriana and Carmela.

from Season Six, in which Vito Spatafore went for a walk in New Hampshire, required the editors to "paint" an entire landscape of snow at his feet.

Once assembled, the editor's cut is sent to the director, who has four days to make changes, and then David Chase goes to work. "To David, editing is really a kind of writing," says Ilene Landress. Chase will often practically reinvent the script. Scenes will be reordered, possibly reshot, or even moved to different episodes. The informal record for number of full versions of an episode, says Smart, is twenty-seven—for the Season Three opener, "Mr. Ruggiero's Neighborhood." Common in film, this level of attention to editing is practically unheard of in television.

One example of how an episode can radically change in editing is "Long Term Parking," the penultimate episode of Season Five in which Adriana is shot. Originally, the show contained a scene in which Christopher goes to Tony and tells him about Adriana's betrayal. "We had shot it and edited it and we thought it was great," says writer Terence Winter. "Then, one day, David calls me and [director] Tim Van Patten and says, 'You know what? I think I'm going to take that scene out.' We were horrified. One, it was one of the best scenes that Michael and Jim had ever done together. Two, I thought we needed it to tell the story. But David said, 'I think it works better without it.'"

As it happened, the tearfully intense scene between Tony and Christopher in Tony's basement was used as a flashback at the beginning of Season Six. And "Long Term Parking," in which Adriana's fate slowly dawned on the audience at the same time it did Adriana, became a masterpiece of suspense. "David's always right," Winter shakes his head. "Every single time I've fought him, gone to the mat, *knowing* that I was right, I was wrong. It's like, 'How the fuck does he know?'"

KEEPING SCORE:
MUSIC ON *THE SOPRANOS*

ONE OF THE MOST DISTINCTIVE ELEMENTS of *The Sopranos* has always been its varied and passionate use of music. David Chase, himself a drummer, made the decision early on that unlike most shows, his would not employ a composer. That meant no soaring strings or "Tony and Carmela's Theme" to help the plot along. Instead, both functions of music—as "source," meaning coming from a realistic place onscreen such as a radio, and "score"—would be fulfilled by existing material. While it's fair to say that Chase exercises control over every aspect of *The Sopranos* production, choosing those songs has become his own particularly special province.

In general, Chase says, he tries to mostly abide by a simple guideline for most of the music: What would Tony listen to? "We use a lot of Tom Petty, Pink Floyd—the kind of seventies rock Tony would have grown up with," he says. But, in fact, the great joy of

the piece, "Seven Souls." "You just needed to know he was talking about death. And resurrection."

Often a song will serve two functions—appearing first in an episode as source music and later as score, to drastically different effect. The Kinks's "Living on a Thin Line," was sexy when Ralphie's stripper girlfriend danced to it in Season Three's "University"; it took on a whole different meaning later, after he had beaten her to death. In another instance, Van Morrison was heard on Tony Blundetto's car stereo singing, "We send you glad tidings from New York," moments before Tony Soprano shot him dead. Interesting, given that Tony was essentially acting on the New York Family's orders; but when the song returned as the score to end the episode, and Season Five, it was Morrison's soaring, valedictory tone that mattered the most. "On another level, that was us—the show—saying goodbye to the audience, because we knew we were taking time off," Chase says. "It was a farewell from this part of the world (New York and New Jersey)."

And then there is that handful of songs that simply seem to sum up the entire show: Nick Lowe's "The Beast in Me," which ended the pilot episode (the brooding Johnny Cash version, Chase says, would have been too portentous for a fledgling show); or The Kinks's "I'm Not Like Everybody Else," played over Tony's triumphant exit from Janice's house after goading her to anger; or Elvis Costello's "Complicated Shadows" with its lyric, "All you

OFTEN A SONG WILL SERVE TWO FUNCTIONS—APPEARING FIRST IN AN EPISODE AS SOURCE MUSIC AND LATER AS SCORE, TO DRASTICALLY DIFFERENT EFFECT.

The Sopranos music is that there are no rules. When you expect a zig, Chase will zag—throwing in a song that seems like it's in direct counterpoint to the action on screen. (Think of the bouncing, Latin-tinged Sinatra song, "Baubles, Bangles and Beads" that Big Pussy throws on the CD player just as the guys are about to confront him on his snitching.) Then, just when you've grown accustomed to irony, Chase plays it dead straight. (Think of Keith Richards's melancholic wail and Charlie Watts's gunshot snare—*crack, crack*—on the Rolling Stones's "Thru and Thru," which ends the same episode.)

At times, we're meant to focus on the lyrics and their literal correspondence to the action. Other times, it's all about mood, like the foreboding growl of William S. Burroughs over music by the band Material, which opened up Season Six. "What mattered there wasn't so much what was being said but the feeling," says Chase of

gangsters and rude clowns/ Who were shooting up the town/ When you should have found someone to put the blame on/ Though the fury's hot and hard/ I still see that cold graveyard/ There's a solitary stone that's got your name on it."

"The fact is we could do the entire show using just the Rolling Stones or Elvis Costello or Bob Dylan and we couldn't go wrong. But it would almost make it too easy. Something like "Complicated Shadows" delivers the mood, the plot, the subtext, everything," Chase says. "So who needs *us*?"

Obviously, Chase is a lover of rock and roll. But he has ranged far and wide in his choice of music—from opera to hip-hop to electronica, even to that most classic producer of "mob hits," Frank Sinatra, while somehow consistently avoiding cliché. "David always surprises me," says Steven Van Zandt, himself no slouch when it comes to eclectic musical taste. "David's always coming up with odd

Dominic Chianese, who plays Uncle Junior, is a real-life guitarist, singer, and even one-time emcee.

choices that work. Who would have thought to use Johnny Thunder as a mob song? Honestly, there's nobody better than David."

Except in rare cases, Chase insists on seeing a full edit of an episode before adding songs, so as not to let the emotional power of music cloud his sense of structure and story. Sometimes, says post-production producer Martin Bruestle, part of whose job it is to work with Chase on each episode's music, "music is not added to the episode until after numerous editorial passes are done. At the beginning of the editorial process, Chase is very interested in story." Behind the producer's office in Los Angeles, there is an ever-growing stack of CDs he refers to as his "Put a Pin in It" pile—Chase's term for songs he's interested in using somewhere down the line. It's not unusual for a song to wait around with a pin in it for several years before finding a home. Chase originally tried to use "Seven Souls" in the pilot. Van Zandt's own "Inside of Me" was tried as a possible accompaniment to the opening credits; it ended up in a slot in the Season One finale.

Songs spotlighted in the end credits or during montages aren't the only ones subjected to a rigorous, not to say obsessive, selection process. Every tune on the car stereo, every seemingly innocuous piece of Muzak in the background, every song accompanying a stripper at the Bada Bing is fussed over. "Let's say there's a scene in the back room of the Bing and you can hear the music through the wall," says Bruestle. "Well, what kind of scene is it? You could do something playful or you could do something ominous and foreboding. Either way, it creates a totally different scene."

"Martin is a genius at this," says Chase. "He helped the show with his subtle choices a million different unsung times."

The Sopranos has scored its share of coups in getting artists to lend their songs to the show. When Led Zeppelin's "Rock and Roll" played in a pizza parlor during Season Three, it was the first time the band had ever licensed to a TV show. Still, some artists are beyond even the reach of the Family. A Beatles song Chase had his heart set on for an episode in Season Six proved too expensive. Citing objections to the show's R-rated content, Bobby McFerrin refused to allow his "Don't Worry Be Happy" to be sung by a Big Mouth Billy Bass mounted singing fish. (The props department ordered a custom fish to sing "YMCA" instead.) For similar reasons, Donna Summer withheld the rights to play "Love to Love You Baby" at the Bada Bing.

There's one more piece to *The Sopranos* music puzzle, and that's the influence of Chase's wife, Denise. Among other picks, it was Denise Chase's idea to combine Henry Mancini's theme from *Peter Gunn* with The Police's "Every Breath You Take" for the memorable opening climax of the Season Two opener. "We were driving somewhere and listening to the radio when The Police song came on. "She gets all the credit for that one," Chase says.

"PINE BARRENS"

AN ORAL HISTORY

DAVID CHASE HAS SAID THAT THE GOAL OF each episode of *The Sopranos* is to function as a mini-movie. Few individual episodes provide a more memorable example of that ethos than Season Three's "Pine Barrens."

The action was simple enough: Tony tells Paulie and Christopher to pick up some money from a Russian mobster for Silvio, who's sick with a virus. Already grumbling, Paulie and Christopher show up and Paulie picks a fight that ends with the Russian apparently dead. The two decide to bury the body in the

Pine Barrens, an enormous tract of woodland in southern New Jersey. When they arrive, the putatively dead Russian hits Christopher with a shovel and takes off, leading the guys on a chase that leaves them lost in the freezing woods. With increasing joy, we proceed to watch them fall apart.

Part *Deliverance*, part *Abbott and Costello Meet the Russian*, part *Blair Witch Project*, and all *Sopranos*, the resulting episode is also a case study in how good television is often a product of both good planning and happy accidents.

"WHAT HAPPENED TO THE RUSSIAN?"

DAVID CHASE: As I remember it, Tim Van Patten had some sort of dream about Paulie and Christopher lost in the forest. You know, two guys from Nutley with their city shoes on, walking around the woods.

TIM VAN PATTEN, DIRECTOR: My father was a horse player and he used to take me and my brother to Atlantic City. On the way down, he'd always try to make an adventure out of it, so we'd stop off at the Pine Barrens. He'd tell us these crazy stories about the Jersey Devil—half-man and half-beast—living in there. It was a spooky place with a kind of magic in it. So, I was lying in bed and I sort of half-dreamed this idea.

TERENCE WINTER, EXECUTIVE PRODUCER: Tim mentioned the idea to me, and I said, "If you don't go into David's office and tell him this, I am going to steal it and go in myself."

Van Patten had his dream during Season Two, but it wasn't until the end of Season Three that the idea fit into the show's plot. Steve Buscemi drew the directing duties, the first of four episodes he'd direct.

STEVE BUSCEMI, DIRECTOR: Originally the idea was that this was going to be an easy episode: The guys go into the woods and it's short and simple. But it turned out to be the first episode that took twelve days to shoot.

CHASE: We had a woods location at the South Mountain Reservation. And at the last minute the Essex County commissioner (who later went to prison for corruption) decided that, because we were a "disgrace to Italians," we would no longer be able to use county streets.

BUSCEMI: We were all ready to shoot and then we lost the location. It was looking pretty grim. We had looked at Harriman State Park across the border in New York before, but they only showed us one spot, which wasn't going to work. Finally, they said this other area in the park was available. It was like our last hope.

PHIL ABRAHAM, DIRECTOR OF PHOTOGRAPHY: When we scouted the location it was as dry and brown and barren as it could be. We talked about what would happen if it snowed. And then just before shooting: four feet of snow. My God, you could never duplicate it. I remember the first shot we did was of the guys just trudging through the snow. It wasn't snowing, but the wind was blowing the snow off of the trees and there were crystals in the air. . . . I mean it was like, *Wow*.

After a cultural misunderstanding, Paulie and Christopher decided to dispose of a Russian criminal.

The guys were out of their element.

WINTER: The snow made it so much more plausible for them to get lost. It was the same everywhere you looked. And Michael and Tony . . . whenever you get the two of them together in a pressurized situation, it's going to be gold.

CHASE: Except for visually, the snow was a disaster! Why couldn't they follow their tracks back to safety? I was going to shoot myself!

MICHAEL IMPERIOLI, CHRISTOPHER: It was a gift. It just made everything so much more alien and foreign for these guys.

TONY SIRICO, PAULIE WALNUTS: It was cold, boy. They did their best to keep us warm but I was still in the snow and my foot was wet. The PAs were always rubbing my feet and picking me up when I fell in the snow. It wasn't the guys either, it was the girl PAs, who picked me up. Oh, I loved it man.

Unexpected snow on location ended up enhancing the episode's power.

Of course, there were other subplots in the episode.

BUSCEMI: Most people remember the episode for the guys being lost, but there was also Meadow catching Jackie Jr. coming out of an apartment with a different girl. And there was Tony and his new girlfriend, Gloria Trillo, who you're starting to figure out is a little crazy. He winds up having to leave her to go get the guys and she throws a steak at him. That was actually me who threw it. Annabella Sciorra couldn't get it right. The prop guy was trying it, finally I was like, "Let me try." Jimmy [Gandolfini] claims I was dying to do it.

And then there was Bobby Bacala, enlisted to help rescue Christopher and Paulie, who reports for duty in full Elmer-Fudd-like hunting regalia.

STEVE SCHIRRIPA, BOBBY: We shot that scene at about seven in the morning and Jim had already seen my outfit.

So I was thinking, *How in the world am I going to make Jim laugh here?* Nothing is funny at 7 A.M. So I went to the prop guy, Anthony, and I got him to give me an assortment of dildos and a dreadlock wig. When they were doing Jim's reaction shot—I was off-camera—I came out with this wig on my head and a two-and-a-half foot dildo swinging out of my pants. Jim almost fell over. If you look, you can see Dominic [Chianese] almost smile, but he doesn't break character. Of course, I never asked why props had all these dicks lying around.

Perhaps the biggest legacy of "Pine Barrens" is what you don't see, i.e., what becomes of the Russian. It has become one of the most tantalizing mysteries in The Sopranos *history.*

WINTER: That's the question I get asked more than any other. It drives people crazy: "Where's the Russian? What happened to the Russian?" We could say, "Well, he got out and there's a big mob war with the Russians," or "He crawled off and died." But we wanted to keep it ambiguous. You know, not everything gets answered in life.

CHASE: They shot a guy. Who knows where he went? Who cares about some Russian? This is what Hollywood has done to America. Do you have to have closure on every little thing? Isn't there any mystery in the world? It's a murky world out there. It's a murky life these guys lead. And by the way, I do know where the Russian is. But I'll never say because so many people got so pissy about it.

One interrupted dinner date later, Tony rescued the guys.

WHAT WE'LL NEVER KNOW

THE CASE OF THE MISSING RUSSIAN IS HARDLY the only plot point to tease, frustrate, and/or confuse fans over the years. In part, this is by design, an aspect of David Chase's philosophy of storytelling. "In life, you don't get an ending to every story," he says. "You can't tie a little ribbon on everything and say it's over. And yeah, I know...'*The Sopranos* isn't life.' But it's *based* on it!"

In fact, most such stories don't so much disappear as go underground for a while, or they fail to be as portentous as they might at first seem. A classic example included Ray Curto, who we learned was a government informer at the beginning of Season Three. What seemed at the time to be a potentially explosive revelation turned out to be nothing of the sort; for the next two seasons we occasionally caught glimpses of Curto on the periphery of Tony's world. Then, at exactly the moment he might have started being of use to the FBI, the character had a heart attack and died. End of story. "We just wanted to give an indication of what life is like for somebody like Tony Soprano. He's constantly talking to people who are rats but *he* doesn't know it," Chase says. "Only people at home waiting for the Russian know it. The reality is that lots of these guys play both sides of the fence and are informing. There are probably several other guys wearing a wire in Tony's family." Chase declines to name names.

Other stories, meanwhile, are really over. Chase says he is surprised to find that, after "Where's the Russian?" the subplot he hears most about is Dr. Melfi's rape. Many viewers are awaiting further development, although the episode, "Employee of the Month," would seem to be neatly self-contained: Melfi is assaulted in her office parking garage. The rapist is caught, but set free on a technicality. Melfi finds herself tempted to seek revenge using Tony, but ultimately decides not to cross that line.

"If you're raised on a steady diet of Hollywood movies and network television, you start to think, *Obviously there's going to be some moral accounting here*," Chase says. "That's not the way the world works. It all comes down to why you're watching. If all you want is to see big Tony Soprano take that guy's head and bang it against the wall like a cantaloupe . . . The point is—Melfi, despite pain and suffering, made her moral, ethical choice and we should applaud her for it. *That's* the story."

THE SOPRANOS

EPISODE GUIDE

Season 1, Episode 1:
"THE SOPRANOS"
Directed by: David Chase
Written by: David Chase

Season 1, Episode 2:
"46 LONG"
Directed by: Daniel Attias
Written by: David Chase

I'M AFRAID I'M GOING TO LOSE MY FAMILY. LIKE I LOST THE DUCKS.
—TONY SOPRANO

AND SO IT BEGINS. TONY SOPRANO, psychologically conflicted boss of northern New Jersey, struck by a panic attack, checks into therapy. He reviews his day with his newfound shrink, Dr. Melfi—recounting "coffee" meetings, family conflicts, and politics, plus a very special flock of ducks. But he's also worried that Uncle Junior's plans to kill off a rival in friend Artie Bucco's restaurant will cause trouble for Artie with the police. His solution: blow up the restaurant. And amidst Tony's efforts to sway his mother to move to a retirement community, he fears that "things are trending downward" in his world, laments the lack of loyalty among his own kind, and (much to his chagrin) goes on the meds.

EAGER FOR MORE RESPECT AND authority, Tony's nephew Christopher and associate Brendan recklessly tread on Uncle Junior's territory. With acting boss Jackie Aprile fighting a losing battle with cancer, tensions in the organization rise. A car theft at A.J.'s school gets Tony and his associates involved, while a kitchen mishap leads Tony to hire some in-home help for his mother, who promptly undermines her son's good intentions. Carmela unwittingly reveals her husband's stress to the wrong source. When Livia drives a car into her best friend, she's finally placed in a posh retirement home very much against her will. In therapy, Tony bristles at the idea that he harbors any ill will

THERE ARE SOME PEOPLE WHO ARE NOT IDEAL CANDIDATES FOR PARENTHOOD.
—DR. JENNIFER MELFI

toward his mother, but outside his sessions oppressive anxiety overcomes him again, as well as the occasional violent outburst.

Season 1, Episode 3:

"DENIAL, ANGER, ACCEPTANCE"

Directed by: Nick Gomez

Written by: Mark Saraceni

Season 1, Episode 4:

"MEADOWLANDS"

Directed by: John Patterson

Written by: Jason Cahill

Season 1, Episode 5:

"COLLEGE"

Directed by: Allen Coulter

Written by: Jim Manos, Jr. and David Chase

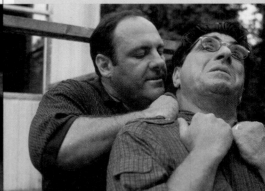

TONY AND COMPANY TAKE ON A JOB with unfamiliar clients in the Hassidic Jewish community and experience an eye-opening

---

I'M A BABBLING IDIOT. THAT'S WHY MY SON PUT ME IN A NURSING HOME.

— LIVIA SOPRANO

---

clash of cultures. Artie and Charmaine Bucco go further into the fold with a catering gig at the Soprano house, just as news of an arson investigation of Vesuvio's restaurant surfaces. Jackie's illness continues to weigh on Tony, while Meadow gets in touch with Christopher looking for a drug hookup. Despite Tony's efforts to placate Uncle Junior and manage Christopher's hubris, deadly revenge is meted out to Brendan.

TONY HAS A LOT ON HIS MIND: HIS friends and family haunt his dreams, along with sexual overtones regarding Dr. Melfi, and some cloak-and-dagger paranoia. A detective in debt looks into the good doctor's personal life and makes a poor decision that eventually reaches Tony's ears. In the schoolyard, and with a little help from his sister, A.J. starts to realize the power of his father's connections in the "waste management" business. But even with increasing anxiety and the loss of a top boss, Jackie Aprile, Tony is

---

HEAR ABOUT THE CHINESE GODFATHER? HE MADE THEM AN OFFER THEY COULDN'T UNDERSTAND.

— UNCLE JUNIOR

---

able to negotiate a kind of peace for now, which leaves him right where he wants to be.

TONY GETS SCHOOLED—TAKING Meadow to visit colleges in pastoral Maine. Shortly into the trip, Meadow flat-out asks Dad if he's in the Mafia, and he begrudgingly concedes some of the less-than-savory sources of his income. The bonding moment eventually leads Meadow to make a confession of her own. Back home Father Phil escapes the rain by dropping in on a sickly Carmela, who's not feeling so bad that she can't spend an intimate, and deeply confessional, night with the priest. A phone call from Dr. Melfi to the Soprano home reveals that Tony's "he" therapist is a "she" and stirs up Carmela's concerns about Tony's infidelity. Up north Tony runs into an old associate with a bad history and literally won't rest until a certain score is settled in a fatal way.

Season 1, Episode 6:
"PAX SOPRANA"

Directed by: Alan Taylor

Written by: Frank Renzulli

Season 1, Episode 7:
"DOWN NECK"

Directed by: Lorraine Senna

Written by: Mitchell Burgess &
Robin Green

Season 1, Episode 8:
"THE LEGEND OF TENNESSEE MOLTISANTI"

Directed by: Tim Van Patten

Written by: Frank Renzulli and
David Chase

JUNIOR HAS FULLY ASSUMED HIS role as boss and is loving it. Asserting his newfound power, he decides to make some new rules—which don't sit so well with some of the capos in the field. As Tony runs interference behind the scenes to keep everyone happy, his dreams feature some very hot-and-bothered interludes with Dr. Melfi. At the same time, the doctor is increasingly aware that the line between her personal and professional lives has become way too blurry. Carmela spends some major cash in a possible bid for Tony's attention, and the killing of a high-earning drug dealer aimed at appeasing Junior leads to further unrest. With the aid of some ancient historical references and a ball game, Tony makes it all good with his uncle and the troops. But then there's his confession of love for his shrink, and the celebration dinner for Junior that's caught on film—by the Feds.

> **I WAS PROUD TO BE JOHNNY SOPRANO'S KID. WHEN HE BEAT THE SHIT OUT OF THAT GUY, I WENT TO THE CLASS, I TOLD THEM HOW TOUGH MY FATHER WAS.**
>
> —TONY SOPRANO

IS HISTORY DOOMED TO REPEAT itself? Does the apple ever far fall from the tree? These questions weigh heavily on Tony's mind as A.J. gets into trouble at school and Tony is moved to reflect on his own complicated, and conflicted, childhood. Memories of pride, shame, and a mother who threatened to stick a fork in his eye invade his thoughts. While A.J. is suspended for a boozy infraction, he makes a daytime visit to his grandmother that results in the disclosure that Tony's in therapy—an idea that Livia quite literally cannot accept. Suspected of having ADD, A.J. is subjected to a battery of tests. Tony has a strong reaction when presented with the borderline results, and Carmela backs him up. No worries: Ice-cream sundaes with whipped cream cure all. For now.

WORD OF PENDING INDICTMENTS IS in the air, and Tony and crew consider taking conveniently-timed "vacations." Instead, they opt for some thorough housecleaning, stashing weapons and cash around town (like in Livia's closet at Green Grove). Christopher suffers a blow to his ego when he's not named as a potential FBI target, and he's also being tormented by dreams of his latest kill, Emil Kolar. Melfi's ex pushes her to confront the truly sinister nature of her mafioso client, and Meadow's getting bolder about discussing dad's business. When Junior pays a visit to Livia, she informs him of Tony's biggest secret: he's seeing a shrink. But things are looking up for Christopher—he finally gets a mention in the papers as a "reputed gangster".

Season 1, Episode 9:

"BOCA"

Directed by: Andy Wolk

Written by: Jason Cahill and
Robin Green & Mitchell Burgess

Season 1, Episode 10:

"A HIT IS A HIT"

Directed by: Matthew Penn

Written by: Joe Bosso and
Frank Renzulli

Season 1, Episode 11:

"NOBODY KNOWS
ANYTHING"

Directed by: Henry J. Bronchtein

Written by: Frank Renzulli

WITH THE THREAT OF FEDERAL INDICT-ments keeping everyone on edge, Junior hightails it to Boca to beat the heat and spend some quality time with his sixteen-year squeeze, Roberta. Unfortunately, what happens between the sheets in Boca doesn't stay in Boca, and news of Junior's "selfless" side in bed reaches the wrong ears up north, undermining his authority. But Tony's trips to the shrink have Junior even more concerned. When the coach of Meadow's winning soccer team decides to relocate, it's a move he's not so subtly discouraged from making by "his friends at the Bada Bing." Then revelations of the coach's off-the-field relationship with Meadow's suicidal friend land him squarely in the literal line of Tony's fire. Getting arrested just might have saved his life.

MY NEPHEW IS SEEING A PSYCHIA-TRIST. IT MAKES ME WANT TO CRY.

—JUNIOR SOPRANO

EVERYBODY'S MAKING NEW FRIENDS. A chance late-night meeting at a burger joint lands Christopher and Adriana at the posh estate of rapper-turned-mogul Massive Genius, who's in search of a favor regarding some long-past business with Hesh Rabkin.

THIS IS ALL A MESSAGE TO YOUR FRIENDS. STAY AWAY FROM PORT NEW-ARK. DON'T EVEN DRIVE OUT TO JERSEY. NOT EVEN ON SUNDAYS.

—PAULIE WALNUTS

When Christopher arranges a sit-down, Massive agrees to provide Adriana with some music biz advice, though he's interested in giving her a bit more than that. A botched demo recording, a smashed guitar, and a reality check later, Adriana is calling it quits with Christopher. At Casa Soprano, Tony and Carmela branch out by hanging with the doctor next door and his country club cronies, but even with the benefit of some hot stock tips, it turns out the price of this membership is way too high.

HOW'S THIS FOR A FOUR-LETTER word: wire. Somebody's wearing one, and Vin Makazian, Tony's cop on the take, says it's Tony's good friend Pussy Bonpensiero. Pussy has got some problems: His back is out and he's slacking off on the job—but would he really take down his friends? Devastated by the idea (and the unavoidable response), Tony pays a visit to the immobile and bathrobe-clad Pussy to remind him of his "options" but leaves feeling his own regarding his friend are running out. Just as Paulie Walnuts is charged with getting some visible proof of Pussy's betrayal, important questions surface regarding Jimmy Altieri's loyalty and the $30K the crooked cop owed Pussy. No use in going to Makazian for any answers: Getting caught up in a bordello bust put him over the edge—of a really high bridge. Livia, meanwhile, has got Junior's ear—about the sale of her house and some of Tony's business at the Green Grove, which only makes for more very bad blood.

Season 1, Episode 12:
"ISABELLA"

Directed by: Allen Coulter

Written by: Robin Green & Mitchell Burgess

Season 1, Episode 13:
"I DREAM OF JEANNIE CUSAMANO"

Directed by: John Patterson

Written by: David Chase

Season 2, Episode 1:
"GUY WALKS INTO A PSYCHIATRIST'S OFFICE"

Directed by: Allen Coulter

Written by: Jason Cahill

WHY THE FUCK WOULD PUSSY RUN?
—CHRISTOPHER MOLTISANTI

PUSSY'S GONE MISSING, AND TONY'S in a bad way, to put it mildly. The only thing that can get him out of bed is Isabella, the fetching Italian dental student staying next door. A shell of a husk of a man, Tony tells Melfi he feels dead inside. The truth is, he's about to feel a lot more dead pretty much everywhere—courtesy of the hit Uncle Junior has out on him. A lunch with Isabella raises his spirits, but as Tony finds out, nothing quite revives your will to live like fending off a couple of "carjackers." A post-incident visit from Livia and Junior shows the first signs of an all-too-convenient bout of senility for Momma Soprano, and the Feds meet with Tony to give him an offer they hope he can't refuse. But really, he's more concerned with knowing if Melfi violated any doctor-patient privilege and realizing that the Italian beauty is a figment of his imagination.

AS TONY'S MOM DESCENDS FURTHER into dementia, she's transferred to the nursing unit, the place she feared most. Still, she's not so far gone that she can't let Artie know the Vesuvio fire was no accident, at which point Artie takes matters, and a gun, into his own hands. One thing everyone can agree upon is that Jimmy Altieri's the rat, and he's dealt with accordingly. Meanwhile, the Feds have more news for Tony, in the form of some very incriminating taped conversations between Livia and Junior. Tony does what he needs to do on all fronts: He takes out the guy who's gonna take him out, comes clean with the crew about his therapy, and tells Melfi to get out of town till things calm down. He also heads to the hospital to confront his mom, but a stroke helps her evade

MY NEPHEW RUNNING THINGS? NOT THAT STRUNZ. NOT IN THIS LIFE.
—UNCLE JUNIOR

death at the hands of her own son. And Junior, Livia's brother-in-law in arms, gets indicted by the Feds.

WITH JUNIOR SPORTING A NEW WARDrobe of institutional orange, Tony's doing his best to manage family affairs without drawing more attention from the FBI. It's challenging: One minute he's taking out rival Phil Parisi, the next he's having yet another panic attack. Meanwhile, lots of old faces are coming by the Soprano house: Pussy shows up in the driveway, telling Tony about a doctor-recommended stay at a Puerto Rico clinic and that Tony's obvious suspicions made him skip town. But now he wants back in. Longlost sister Janice also returns, bringing with her the need for a place to stay and a well-timed interest in her mother's assets. Christopher is installed as the SEC compliance manager of a crooked stock-trading venture through no skill of his own, and his preoccupation with nose candy only causes more agita for Tony. Poor Dr. Melfi has been forced to run her practice out of a motel room, and Tony's out-of-the-blue assurance that it's safe to go home, as well as his sudden appearance at a diner, infuriate his shrink even more.

Season 2, Episode 2:
"DO NOT RESUSCITATE"

Directed by: Martin Bruestle

Written by: Robin Green & Mitchell Burgess, and Frank Renzulli

Season 2, Episode 3:
"TOODLE-FUCKING-OO"

Directed by: Lee Tamahori

Written by: Frank Renzulli

Season 2, Episode 4:
"COMMENDATORI"

Directed by: Tim Van Patten

Written by: David Chase

TONY MAKES A POWER PLAY AGAINST Junior, who swears from behind bars that Livia had nothing to do with the attempted hit on his nephew. He just wants Tony to make peace with his mother. Racial tensions run high at a construction site, and the Soprano crew is brought in to mediate with swinging bats and fists. Janice continues to grease the self-serving wheels regarding Livia's affairs, but already she's remembering why she left home in the first place. And a late-night visit to Grandma finds A.J. asking Livia what DNR means. (She knows: "Do not resuscitate.") When Junior gets out of the clink courtesy of medical leave, he's put under house arrest, but he's determined to stay in the game by conducting business from his doctor's office.

TONY IS ... AFRAID TO LEAVE NEW JERSEY AND HE'S THREATENED BY ANYBODY WHO'S BROKEN FREE.

— JANICE SOPRANO

TONY AND CARMELA WRESTLE WITH the task of raising a teenage girl, and it's particularly hard when the adolescent in question knows how to play her parents like a pro. Janice offers unsolicited child-rearing

SUCKIN' UP TO TONY SOPRANO HAS DONE WONDERS FOR YOU.

— RICHIE APRILE

advice but changes her tune of tolerance when Meadow's party at Livia's house ends up trashing the place. Richie Aprile, brother of former boss Jackie, gets out of prison and wastes no time wreaking havoc on Tony's turf while also making sure Junior knows Richie's ultimate loyalty is to him. Meanwhile, Jennifer Melfi runs into Tony during a night out and utters this episode's titular phrase, which she sees as the choice of a child—one who's trying to skirt the responsibility of abandoning a patient.

TONY'S HEADED TO THE HOMELAND. The business of moving high-end hot cars takes him and his associates to Italy for some dealings with distant family. Tony expects to meet with a legendary boss, but he finds the real power rests with the wife of a player who's not coming home anytime soon. Reeling from the idea that a woman is running the show, Tony comes to learn just how powerful she is. After some negotiation, he settles on a deal that gives her a significant discount and him a new soldier, Furio, to take home. Janice and Richie Aprile reignite their romance from twenty years ago, and Pussy's relationship with wife Angie hits the skids when she wants to call it quits. While Pussy is off killing a possible witness to his ongoing betrayal, Carmela reevaluates her own marriage as she counsels Angie on the sins of divorce.

Season 2, Episode 5:

"BIG GIRLS DON'T CRY"

Directed by: Tim Van Patten
Written by: Terence Winter

Season 2, Episode 6:

"THE HAPPY WANDERER"

Directed by: John Patterson
Written by: Frank Renzulli

Season 2, Episode 7:

"D-GIRL"

Directed by: Allen Coulter
Written by: Todd A. Kessler

FORGET YOUR ENEMIES. YOU CAN'T EVEN DEPEND ON YOUR FRIENDS.

—BIG PUSSY BONPENSIERO

EVER THE SUPPORTIVE GIRLFRIEND, Adriana gives Christopher the gift of a class: Acting for Writers. All seems to be going well, until a scene from *Rebel Without a Cause* causes Christopher to fly into a rage and pummel a guy on the stage, and literally trash all of his writing efforts. Dr. Melfi's getting into it with her own therapist, who suggests that Jennifer gets a thrill out of seeing a patient who operates outside the law. In the end, she calls Tony and says she'll take him back. Eventually, he shows up—probably because he feels as if he's losing his temper and mind all too frequently. Some late-night visits to Hesh reveal Tony's father was no stranger to panic attacks either. Furio lands stateside and proves he's up to any task. And more internal movements in the hierarchy push Pussy farther from the center of power; he consoles himself by talking to his FBI contact.

DAVEY SCATINO, THE FATHER OF A friend of Meadow's, wants in on some of Tony's action—specifically, some high-stakes card games. There's just one problem: He's got a bit of a gambling addiction and is already into Richie Aprile for eight large. A friendly appeal to Tony gets him into the ultraexclusive "executive game," but it also lands him in even more serious debt. When Tony is forced to become enforcer, Scatino hands over his kids' Jeep as partial payment and it ends up in the Soprano garage as a gift to Meadow—who recognizes it instantly. Junior's sharing all kinds of info with Tony,

NOW THAT YOU FOUND OUT THAT YOU HAVE A RETARDED FAMILY MEMBER, DO YOU FEEL BETTER ABOUT COMING HERE?

—DR. JENNIFER MELFI

like the fact that Livia is hardly strapped for cash and the existence of a retarded uncle in the family. And Richie? He's still challenging Tony and it doesn't look like he'll stop anytime soon.

HOORAY FOR HOLLYWOOD. OR NOT. Amy, the fiancée of Christopher's cousin, comes to town on business for her job as a development exec for Jon Favreau's company. She's hot to read the script she's heard about and introduce Christopher to Jon. A visit to an N.Y.C. set—featuring cameos by Sandra Bernhardt and Janeane Garofalo—makes quite an impression on the Jersey boy, and things look promising as he noshes pizza with Favreau and Amy, offering insights into his "world." But after getting some writing advice and hotel suite action from Amy, Christopher discovers his newfound L.A. friends are screwing him in more ways than one. And when Tony finds out about his nephew's new cinematic distraction, he demands Christopher choose where his true loyalty lies. Pussy asks himself the same questions and is crumbling under the weight of his betrayal, while A.J. has discovered Nietzsche and becomes an existentialist.

Season 2, Episode 8:

"FULL LEATHER JACKET"

Directed by: Allen Coulter

Written by: Robin Green & Mitchell Burgess

Season 2, Episode 9:

"FROM WHERE TO ETERNITY"

Directed by: Henry J. Bronchtein

Written by: Michael Imperioli

Season 2, Episode 10:

"BUST OUT"

Directed by: John Patterson

Written by: Frank Renzulli and Robin Green & Mitchell Burgess

MEADOW IS INCREASINGLY FIXATED on attending Berkeley. That's a little too far away for Carmela, so with hopes of increasing her daughter's chances at Georgetown, she approaches neighbor Jean Cusamano about getting a letter of recommendation from Jean's sister, an alum of the D.C.-based school. Some initial resistance lands Carmela in the sister's office with a pineapple ricotta pie and a not so subtle demand that the letter happen. Christopher shows up at Adriana's house with an apology, an engagement ring, and the resolution to clean up his act and refocus—a trajectory that's cut short when two young turks decide to take Christopher down as a "favor" for Richie Aprile. When the smoke clears, Christopher is shot, one kid is dead, but the other, Matt Bevilaqua, is missing. Meanwhile, Richie kisses up to Tony by giving him the leather jacket he took off of Rocco DiMeo when he whacked him back in the day. When Tony gives away the jacket, Richie takes it as an insult of the highest order.

I'M DRAGGING A BUNCH OF FUCKING GHOULS AROUND WITH ME AND MIKEY'S THEIR FUCKING RINGLEADER.

—PAULIE WALNUTS

THINGS ARE SERIOUS WITH CHRIStopher. He's in ICU, and cardiac arrest leaves him clinically dead for a whole minute. He returns from his brief trip to the other side convinced he's going to hell and carrying a cryptic message from Mikey for Tony and Paulie Walnuts. Paulie's more than a little bit spooked—that's Mikey Palmice, the guy he whacked ages ago. Paulie enlists the help of a priest, a psychic, and more to figure out if he's really going to burn forever. When Dr. Melfi passes judgment on Tony she becomes concerned for her safety. Meanwhile, Carmela's had it with Tony's *goomaras* and demands that at the very least he undergo a "snip" to avoid an illegitimate Soprano. Pussy gets a tip regarding the whereabouts of Christopher's assailant on the lam, and in a crucial and well-timed display of loyalty to Tony, he joins the boss for a payback killing.

THE BEVILAQUA MURDER WASN'T as clean as it should've been. Turns out there was an eyewitness, and Tony preps for the worst, stashing $400K for Carmela with his lawyer and letting Dr. Melfi know he might be going away "for a very long time." Despite his good intentions, Tony misses A.J.'s last swim meet of the season, and Carmela is fed up with his neglect of the family. Her frustration finds her locking lips with Vic Musto, an attractive contractor who is wallpapering her bathroom and who also happens to be the brother-in-law of Davey Scatino. A scheduled lunch date between the two promises to involve more than just pasta and vino, until Vic learns Tony has bankrupted his nephew's college fund, and he leaves Carmela in the lurch. Richie continues to make trouble, telling Junior that Tony needs to be taken out once and for all, while Pussy's FBI contact demands he get a rock-solid confession of the Bevilaqua hit on tape. Things look bad for Tony and he knows it, but when his crime's key witness suddenly backs off, he dodges yet another bullet.

Season 2, Episode 11:

"HOUSE ARREST"

Directed by: Tim Van Patten

Written by: Terence Winter

Season 2, Episode 12:

"THE KNIGHT IN WHITE SATIN ARMOR"

Directed by: Allen Coulter

Written by: Robin Green & Mitchell Burgess

Season 2, Episode 13:

"FUNHOUSE"

Directed by: John Patterson

Written by: David Chase and Todd A. Kessler

AFTER TONY IS GRANTED A REPRIEVE by the fates, his lawyer advises him to distance himself from family dealings and spend some time at his legitimate businesses. He takes an office at Barone Sanitation and is quickly bored to tears, but he also learns that Richie is selling drugs on a route and putting everyone in jeopardy. When Tony confronts Aprile and demands an end to it, Richie claims backing from Junior on the scheme. The stress is getting to Tony; he breaks out in a rash and is felled by yet another anxiety attack. Dr. Melfi is feeling the heat too and is calming her nerves with frequent shots of vodka between sessions. Soon she's on the meds as well. Junior finds comfort with a lady friend from his past, and Janice and Richie go house-hunting. But Richie's also looking for trouble: He's caught on tape making his drug rounds in blatant defiance of Tony's wishes.

WHAT, DID YOU TAKE A SLEDGE HAMMER TO MY BALLS?

—UNCLE JUNIOR

TONY ENDS THE AFFAIR WITH HIS *goomara* Irina, but she's not going quietly, and as threatened, tries to kill herself. Meanwhile, Pussy's confusing his role as informant with being a crime-fighting employee of the FBI, and he goes all out to work with the Feds and bust his friends. After careful consideration of his alliances and best interests, Junior lets Tony know that Richie has got a bullet with his name on it. An engagement party at the Soprano house for Janice and Richie gives the impression of a match made in heaven, but a fight back at the lovebirds' house ends with Janice sending Richie straight to hell—with a bullet to the heart.

WITH RIVAL RICHIE APRILE OUT OF the way and renewed passion between Carmela and Tony, things are finally looking up. But when Livia gets busted at the airport with a stolen ticket, the FBI moves in with some charges they hope will finally stick—thirty to life. A bad case of food poisoning sends Tony to bed, and his dreams force him to admit the truth he's known all along: Pussy's a rat. A trip to his good friend's house confirms Tony's suspicions once and for all, and he wastes no time in sending Pussy to sleep with the fishes.

NOT IN THE FACE OKAY? YOU GIVE ME THAT? HUH? KEEP MY EYES?

—BIG PUSSY BONPENSIERO

Season 3, Episode 1:
"MR. RUGGERIO'S NEIGHBORHOOD"
Directed by: Allen Coulter
Written by: David Chase

Season 3, Episode 2:
"PROSHAI, LIVUSHKA"
Directed by: Tim Van Patten
Written by: David Chase

Season 3, Episode 3:
"FORTUNATE SON"
Directed by: Henry J. Bronchtein
Written by: Todd A. Kessler

THE FBI IS STEPPING UP ITS GAME and concocts an elaborate plan to bug the Soprano home. An army of agents tails every member of the family, as well as maid Liliana, while a team infiltrates the household to set the trap. Tony grows concerned that Patsy Parisi, a recent import from Junior's crew, might have an inkling that Tony killed his twin brother, and it turns out he's right.

HELLO. GOD DON'T TRANSFER ME NOW. ADRIANA LA CERVA. HOW GREEN WAS MY FUCKING VALLEY.
— FBI AGENT, LOOKING AT ADRIANA'S ASS WITH BINOCULARS

Meadow settles in at Columbia, and a family plumbing emergency demands that Tony and Carmela return to the house unexpectedly, setting back the Feds' operation for the time being.

I'M GLAD SHE'S DEAD. NOT JUST GLAD—I WISHED SHE'D DIE.
— TONY SOPRANO

TONY HIRES IRINA'S RUSSIAN FRIEND Svetlana to give his mom some in-home care, but her services are short-lived when Livia dies of a massive stroke in bed. Janice returns from Seattle for the funeral and a chance to locate her mother's rumored stash of bills, and she insists on orchestrating a tender remembrance of Mom. The problem is, nobody's got anything good to say. In therapy, Tony's quick to declare that he's glad Livia's dead, citing that, for starters, now she won't be testifying against him in court. With Richie Aprile gone into "witness protection," ambitious Ralphie Cifaretto has taken over the dead man's territory. Ralphie makes it clear to Tony he wants to be made captain, and soon. When Meadow brings home a new boyfriend who's Jewish and African American, Tony expresses his displeasure in no uncertain terms.

CHRISTOPHER'S TIME HAS COME: He's a made man. But things get tense when the sports ring he inherits with his new status underperforms and he's caught $2K short on his kick-up to Paulie. As promised to his dead friend Jackie Aprile, Tony meets with Jackie Jr. to say his dad never wanted him involved with the business, but Jackie's already giving helpful tips to Christopher about a box office heist at Rutgers. In a bid to get back some of her mom's old records from Svetlana, Janice takes the Russian's fake leg and invites consequences. Tony has a therapeutic breakthrough, remembering the origin of his panic attacks: the day he witnessed his dad chop off the pinkie of a butcher in serious debt. A.J. determines he doesn't want to go to college after all, and he makes good on the football team when he's named defensive captain, an honor that promptly causes him to pass out on the field.

...SO MAY YOUR SOUL BURN IN HELL IF YOU BETRAY YOUR FRIENDS IN THE FAMILY.
— TONY SOPRANO

Season 3, Episode 4:
"EMPLOYEE OF THE MONTH"

Directed by: John Patterson

Written by: Robin Green & Mitchell Burgess

Season 3, Episode 5:
"ANOTHER TOOTHPICK"

Directed by: Jack Bender

Written by: Terence Winter

Season 3, Episode 6:
"UNIVERSITY"

Directed by: Allen Coulter

Teleplay by: Terence Winter and Salvatore J. Stabile

Story by: David Chase & Terence Winter & Todd A. Kessler and Robin Green & Mitchell Burgess

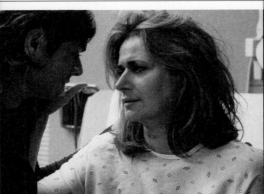

RALPHIE CIFARETTO GETS INVOLVED with Rosalie Aprile and takes her son Jackie Jr. under his wing—and on a business-related beat-down, a move he knows will anger Tony. Janice is forced to hand over Svetlana's fake leg when she's attacked by some Russian gangsters. The Newark waterfront development project is funded to the tune of $25 million, and it's sure to be a cash cow for the Jersey organization, but Johnny Sack has just moved over state lines into Tony's territory and may be thinking about more than landscaping decisions. Dr. Melfi finally decides she shouldn't continue treating Tony and resolves to pass him off to a behavioral therapist. But when she is brutally assaulted leaving her office one night and the justice system fails to punish her attacker, her only source of comfort is in knowing she could exact revenge with the help of a certain "sociopathic" patient if she wanted.

CARMELA MAKES AN APPEARANCE with Tony in therapy and the results are anything but healing. On the car ride home from the session, Tony gets a speeding ticket, and then sees to it that the cop who gave it to him

---

MAYBE YOU PASS OUT BECAUSE YOU'RE GUILTY OVER SOMETHING.

— CARMELA SOPRANO

---

gets transferred, a decision he later regrets. Bobby Bacala Sr. comes out of retirement for one last hit, and it's not his terminal cancer that gets him in the end but an accident on the highway leaving the scene of the crime. When Adriana quits her hostess gig at Vesuvio, Artie Bucco is moved to reveal his true, deep feelings for her; his decision to go into business with Tony prompts Charmaine to finally call the whole marriage off. At a doctor's office meeting, Tony learns why Uncle Junior hasn't been acting like himself lately: He's got cancer. In the Soprano house, the FBI wiretap has been "neutralized": Meadow's taken the Feds' lamp to Columbia.

TRACEE, A DANCER AT BADA BING, IS making needy overtures to Tony despite instructions from management that her only relationship with the boss be professional. Her relationship with Ralphie Cifaretto, however, lands her in the family way, and she's not showing up for work at the Bing. Meadow and boyfriend Noah are increasingly intimate—the kind of closeness that involves condoms. So much for young love: He unceremoniously dumps her in the library. When Tracee is dragged back to work, she insults Ralphie in front of the guys, and he exacts deadly revenge when she steps outside for a smoke. When Tony discovers her body out back and Ralphie has nothing to offer but

---

I HAVE COME TO RECLAIM ROME FOR MY PEOPLE.

— RALPHIE CIFARETTO

---

flip comments, Tony breaks code by hitting another made guy, pummelling the insolent Cifaretto to a bloody pulp.

Season 3, Episode 7:
"SECOND OPINION"
Directed by: Tim Van Patten

Written by: Lawrence Konner

Season 3, Episode 8:
"HE IS RISEN"
Directed by: Allen Coulter

Written by: Robin Green & Mitchell Burgess and Todd A. Kessler

Season 3, Episode 9:
"THE TELLTALE MOOZADELL"
Directed by: Daniel Attias

Written by: Michael Imperioli

JUNIOR UNDERGOES SURGERY FOR his stomach cancer, but when it seems he may need yet another operation, Tony insists his uncle get a second opinion. Junior, however, wonders if his nephew might be trying to hasten the old man's death. After his first chemotherapy treatment against his doctor's advice, Junior persists in trying to get his doctor's help, but neither his, nor Tony's, phone calls get returned. Some persuasion from Furio makes him more attentive than ever. Carmela takes a referral from Dr. Melfi for a therapist of her own and is confronted with her complicity in all that Tony does, as well as the directive to end her marriage. Christopher continues to endure a trial by fire at the hands of mentor Paulie Walnuts, who has learned to take great pleasure in humiliating his new soldier. Meanwhile, Angie Bonpensiero is shaking down Tony for more financial support, but when Tony lays his eyes on her new Cadillac, she's busted, as is the car's windshield.

TONY'S HAD JUST ABOUT ALL HE CAN take of Ralphie Cifaretto. He can't forgive him for killing Tracee, the dancer who reminds him of his own little girl, and Ralphie still has a beef with Tony for laying a hand on him. All-out war seems imminent, but the sudden death of Gigi Gestone presents Tony with the opportunity to make peace by promoting Ralphie, which seems to ease tensions, at least temporarily. Meadow is spending more and more quality time with Jackie Jr., and it's a union that thrills Rosalie Aprile but causes Carmela concern. Tony's got his own budding romance with Gloria Trillo, a fellow patient of Dr. Melfi's. When he drops by the Mercedes dealership where she works, they go for a test drive on the road and between the sheets.

I'M TRYING TO QUIT SMOKING.
— TONY SOPRANO

SERIAL KILLER.
I MURDERED SEVEN RELATIONSHIPS.
— GLORIA TRILLO

MEADOW AND JACKIE JR. CONTINUE to be hot and heavy, and by all appearances he seems to be a perfect gentleman. Thing is, he's ditching pre-med, setting up his own crew, and offering protection to a drug dealer at Crazy Horse, the new club Christopher is financing for Adriana. Despite warnings from Christopher to cease and desist, some Ecstasy deals go down in the Crazy Horse parking lot, and when Furio finds out, he sends a message by sending Jackie's partner to the hospital. A.J.'s acting out again, getting busted with some friends for breaking into the school, trashing a trophy case, and tossing furniture into the pool. Tony is a bit distracted from domestic issues, however, because of his intensifying affair with Gloria, who's unlike any of his previous girls on the side. There is one distressing similarity, however: She tried to kill herself when her last relationship went south. When Tony finds Jackie Jr. gambling, he tosses him from the casino, but not before issuing the kid a stern warning to "smarten up."

Season 3, Episode 10:
"...TO SAVE US ALL FROM SATAN'S POWER..."

Directed by: Jack Bender

Written by: Robin Green & Mitchell Burgess

Season 3, Episode 11:
"PINE BARRENS"

Directed by: Steve Buscemi

Teleplay by: Terence Winter

Story by: Tim Van Patten & Terence Winter

Season 3, Episode 12:
"AMOUR FOU"

Directed by: Tim Van Patten

Teleplay by: Frank Renzulli

Story by: David Chase

ALL I KNOW ABOUT THIS GUY IS HE DRIVES A LIVERY CAB, HE WASN'T VERY NICE TO SOMEONE IMPORTANT TO ME.
— TONY SOPRANO

THE HOLIDAYS HAVE ARRIVED IN JER-sey, and the ghosts of Christmas past are haunting Tony. His visions land him back on Dr. Melfi's couch, but he's also still having issues with Jackie Jr., who just doesn't seem to want to listen. Janice attempts to host Christmas dinner while managing her relationship with her new narcoleptic musician boyfriend. Bobby Bacala is persuaded to don the Santa suit traditionally worn by the now-departed Pussy, and Tony and Furio deliver a holiday greeting to Igor, the Russian who roughed up Janice.

PAULIE AND CHRISTOPHER ARE assigned do a no-brainer collection from a Russian named Valery, and it goes horribly awry. When Paulie and the Russian have words, a fight ensues, and pretty soon Tony's deputies are talking about burying the body in the Pine Barrens of Jersey. The thing is, Valery's not one-hundred percent dead yet, and when he fights back Russian-commando-style, Christopher and Paulie are left stunned and bleeding. They've lost Valery, and now they've lost the car. A cell-phone call to Tony elicits little sympathy and the order to track down Valery, as he's connected to a key money-laundering associate. Tony's got other things to think about, like the intoxicat-

WE TAKE HIM IN THE WOODS, DIG A HOLE, END OF STORY.
— PAULIE WALNUTS

ing Gloria Trillo, who is starting to show the darker side of her passionate nature. Meadow's got relationship problems, too: Jackie Jr. is sneaking off to see other girls, and she's onto him.

TONY'S GOT IT BAD FOR GLORIA, AND that ain't good—especially because she's upping the crazy factor. When Carmela takes her wagon in for some work at Globe Mercedes, she's offered a ride home by charming saleswoman "Trillo," and she even receives a thoughtful follow-up call pitching the idea of buying a new car. Tony's not amused, and when he confronts Gloria, things get violent quick. He's seen her mix of self-pity and vindictiveness before—in his mother. Tony calls off the affair, and Patsy Parisi makes it clear there will be deadly consequences should she go near his boss again. In a rash bid to up his status, Jackie Jr. recruits some friends to make a hit on a card game, and things go terribly wrong: Christopher is at the game, Furio gets shot, and the dealer is killed. Christopher wants immediate retribution, but after weighing the politics, Tony says it's Ralphie's place to decide what's next for Jackie Jr.

Season 3, Episode 13:

"THE ARMY OF ONE"

Directed by: John Patterson

Written by: David Chase &
Lawrence Konner

Season 4, Episode 1:

"FOR ALL DEBTS PUBLIC AND PRIVATE"

Directed by: Allen Coulter

Written by: David Chase

Season 4, Episode 2:

"NO-SHOW"

Directed by: John Patterson

Written by: Terence Winter and
David Chase

YOU KNOW, WE NEVER DISCUSSED EXACTLY WHAT YOU WANT FOR YOUR CHILDREN.

—DR. JENNIFER MELFI

I DON'T WANT 'EM TO END UP IN BOONTON WITH THEIR FACE BLOWN OFF...

—TONY SOPRANO

A.J. GETS CAUGHT CHEATING ON AN exam and gets expelled, and Tony's solution to his son's behavior is to send him off to military school. Paulie's soured on Tony due to a money decision that went Ralphie's way, and now Paulie is getting cozy with Johnny Sack. Adriana makes a new friend who just happens to work for the FBI, and Meadow's waxing philosophical about la Vita Soprano. Jackie Jr. goes into hiding in the projects, but he can only run for so long, and ultimately a bullet finds the back of his head.

MONEY'S GETTING TIGHT ALL AROUND. Junior's facing a million dollars in legal fees for his upcoming trial, and he tells Tony he needs to renegotiate their split on earnings; after all, he's the one paying the price for taking the heat. After seeing Angie Bonpensiero hawking sausage at the supermarket, Carmela's concerned about her own financial security and pushes Tony to do some estate planning. Tony's taken to hiding fistfuls of cash in bags of birdseed out back and putting the screws to his capos to create some more income. Despite recent tensions with Christopher, Tony works to get closer to his nephew. He starts by giving Christopher the chance to

YOU NEVER KNOW, I COULD BE ON THE ENDANGERED SPECIES LIST.

—CHRISTOPHER MOLTISANTI

avenge his father's death. And the FBI is closing in on the Soprano family: A flirty nurse at Junior's doctor's office turns out to be an agency plant, and "Danielle" is fast becoming Adriana's new best friend.

WITH PAULIE IN JAIL ON A GUN charge, Christopher is bumped up to acting capo of Paulie's crew. But his decision to boost some fiber-optic cable from the construction site of a high-priced job draws Tony's ire. Silvio undermines Christopher's authority by OK'ing yet another heist. All the responsibility is getting to Christopher, and he's easing the stress by shooting up. Meadow, still reeling from Jackie Jr.'s death, is threatening to drop out of school and take off to Europe. And Janice and Ralphie are now officially an item. Adriana breaks off her relationship with Danielle when she thinks her friend made a play for Christopher. But the true nature of their friendship is revealed when Adriana's picked up by the FBI and told she'll be locked up on drug charges unless she becomes an informant. She doesn't take the news well: Her initial response is one of projectile vomit.

Season 4, Episode 3:
"CHRISTOPHER"

Directed by: Tim Van Patten
Teleplay by: Michael Imperioli
Story by: Michael Imperioli and
Maria Laurino

Season 4, Episode 4:
"THE WEIGHT"

Directed by: Jack Bender
Written by: Terence Winter

Season 4, Episode 5:
"PIE-O-MY"

Directed by: Henry J. Bronchtein
Written by: Robin Green &
Mitchell Burgess

WHEN NEWS OF A NATIVE AMER-ican-led protest of Columbus Day comes to Newark, Italian pride—and tempers—flare. After a violent clash at a pre-parade rally lands Patsy Parisi in jail and fans the flames of conflict, Silvio pressures Tony to take a stand on the issue. But Tony's efforts fall flat, and he ends up being played by a slick Native American casino owner. When Bobby Bacala's wife, Karen, suddenly dies in a car crash, the Soprano women are moved by the grief of a man who was actually devoted to his spouse. The contrast between Bobby and Ralphie is too much for Janice to take, and she kicks her new lover to the curb. And even though he's behind bars, Paulie's still building alliances, filling in Johnny Sack on a particularly disparaging joke made at the expense of the New York boss's wife.

MAYBE WE GOTTA JUST WHACK THIS PRICK.

—SILVIO DANTE

RALPHIE MAKES ONE CRACK ABOUT Ginny Sacrimoni and all hell breaks loose. The word is out that the hurtful remark has reached Johnny Sack's ears, and when Ralphie calls Sack in an attempt to smooth things over, John's even more enraged. After two sit-downs involving top bosses Carmine Lupertazzi and Junior, Johnny's still not satisfied, so he orders Ralphie taken out. Meanwhile Carmine, unimpressed by his deputy's irrationality, puts a hit on Johnny. In the end, it's Gini's passion for Twix that foils both murderous plans. On the domestic front, Carmela has finally persuaded Tony to hire a financial planner, and she's getting serious about a career in real estate. But she's also got something else on her mind—namely, Italian import Furio, who seems to feel the same way. Back at school, Meadow exposes herself to truth and justice, volunteering at the South Bronx Poverty Law Center.

I WOULD FOLLOW (TONY) INTO HELL.

—CHRISTOPHER MOLTISANTI

TONY'S GOT A NEW LOVE INTEREST... of the equine variety. When he pays a few visits to the track to see Ralphie's horse Pie-O-My run and win, it's not long before he's smitten. Tony's accountant is advising his client to steer clear of an estate trust, namely because it's irrevocable in the face of things like divorce. Adriana's doing everything she can to shield herself from anything of interest to the Feds, but that becomes more difficult when Ralphie, and then Tony, start using Crazy Horse as a place to discuss business. Resolved to get herself a decent man, Janice aggressively moves in on the still-grieving Bobby. When some unpaid vet bills prevent Pie-O-My from receiving some badly needed treatment, Ralphie passes off the problem to Tony, who heads out into a storm to help save his newest responsibility.

Season 4, Episode 6:

"EVERYBODY HURTS"

Directed by: Steve Buscemi
Written by: Michael Imperioli

Season 4, Episode 7:

"WATCHING TOO MUCH TELEVISION"

Directed by: John Patterson
Teleplay by: Terence Winter and Nick Santora
Story by: David Chase & Robin Green & Mitchell Burgess & Terence Winter

Season 4, Episode 8:

"MERGERS AND ACQUISITIONS"

Directed by: Daniel Attias
Teleplay by: Lawrence Konner
Story by: David Chase & Robin Green & Mitchell Burgess & Terence Winter

TONY DECIDES TO BRING CHRISTO-pher into his inner circle, telling his nephew they share the sacred bond of family blood. A business opportunity with Frenchman Jean-Phillippe finds Artie Bucco looking for a short-term loan, and Tony insists he front his friend the cash. Tony has learned that Gloria Trillo hung herself, and he erupts in a fit of

WHAT THE FUCK AM I, A TOXIC PERSON OR SOMETHIN'?

—TONY SOPRANO

guilty rage at Dr. Melfi for keeping it from him. Meanwhile, Adriana and Christopher are now on the nod more often than they're not. When Artie goes to collect his money, he's told the cash isn't there and it's never showing up. Despondent, he overdoses on pills and calls Tony, who's not about to have another suicide on his hands. When Tony forgives Artie the debt and has his tab at Vesuvio cleared for the favor, his friend accuses Tony of being a vicious opportunist—and Tony's not so sure he's wrong.

AN OFFHAND REMARK FROM CARMELA'S cousin Brian, the family's new financial adviser, leads Tony and Assemblyman Ron Zellman to partner on a lucrative Housing and Urban Development (HUD) scam. When some entrenched crack addicts prevent Tony and crew from stripping the properties for valuable scrap, a few kids from downtown Newark are enlisted to evict them with gunfire. A handsome profit is made by all involved, but money can't solve everything. Zellman's confession to Tony that he's taken up with Irina ends with Tony stopping by and literally whipping the assemblyman into submission. Thanks to some late-night television, Adriana becomes convinced that as Christopher's wife she can't be forced to testify against him. Soon she's shopping for a dress, but she later learns her information might be faulty. Paulie Walnuts is out of jail, and now he's talking to Johnny Sack about his beefs with Tony, in person.

TONY MEETS RALPHIE CIFARETTO'S latest female companion, art dealer Valentina La Paz, and he approves—probably a little too much. When he pays her a visit to discuss a portrait of Pie-O-My, they waste no time getting to the real business at hand, in a hotel room. Valentina's interested in Tony, but he's got reservations about "going where Ralph Cifaretto's been." But Valentina says actual intercourse isn't exactly Ralphie's thing. A trip to Janice for confirmation and a $3,000 bribe later, Tony's back in the saddle with Valentina. His new romance has not gone undetected by Carmela, who found a telling fake nail on Tony's bedside table as well as the money he has stashed out back, which

ALL HE WANTED ME TO DO WAS DRIP CANDLE WAX ON HIS BALLS.

—VALENTINA LA PAZ

she's taken upon herself to invest. At Green Grove, Paulie's mother is boxed out by some octogenarian politics, a matter Paulie resolves by roughing up a fellow resident's son.

Season 4, Episode 9:
"WHOEVER DID THIS"
Directed by: Tim Van Patten

Written by: Robin Green &
Mitchell Burgess

Season 4, Episode 10:
"THE STRONG, SILENT TYPE"
Directed by: Alan Taylor

Teleplay by: Terence Winter and
Robin Green & Mitchell Burgess

Story by: David Chase

Season 4, Episode 11:
"CALLING ALL CARS"
Directed by: Tim Van Patten

Teleplay by: David Chase & Robin
Green & Mitchell Burgess and
David Flebotte

Story by: David Chase & Robin Green &
Mitchell Burgess & Terence Winter

NOBODY KNOWS WHAT THE FUTURE HOLDS, MY FRIEND.
—PAULIE WALNUTS

AFTER TUMBLING DOWN THE STAIRS of the courthouse, Junior hatches a plan to avoid prosecution due to mental incompetency, and he gets to work studying how to convincingly fake senility. When Ralphie's son, Justin, is in a serious accident on his dad's watch, it seems that Cifaretto might be changing his selfish ways. But when an electrical fire at the stables leads to Pie-O-My being put down, Tony thinks that after the $200K insurance policy he and Ralphie recently took out on the horse, the fire might be a little too well timed. A visit to Ralphie's house confirms Tony's suspicions, and Ralphi ends up dead on his kitchen floor. Tony turns to Christopher for help in cleaning up his mess and is furious when his nephew shows up high—again. Still, the two chop Ralphie into half a dozen pieces and make him disappear.

TONY'S TRYING TO TRACK DOWN Ralphie and—guess what?—he's not answering his phone. His crew's not so sure the boss didn't get too worked up over a pet. Furio reluctantly distances himself from Carmela, while she comes clean to Rosalie Aprile about the intensity of her feelings for him. Dr. Melfi observes that Tony only grieves over the loss of animals, and Christopher is taking out a four-footed friend himself—by sitting on Adriana's dog when he's high. When Christopher gives his fiancée a black eye, it's the last straw and an intervention is scheduled, but the gathering takes a judgmental turn, and Christopher ends up in the hospital. Realizing a dime bag could jeopardize his entire operation, Tony orders Christopher to rehab. Johnny Sack demands a cut of the HUD deal profits. Tony flatly refuses him, but Johnny's not about to take no for an answer.

AFTER A DAYTIME INTERLUDE WITH Svetlana on Junior's couch, Tony's rebuffed by the Russian, who informs the boss she doesn't want to "prop him up." It all makes Tony think this therapy thing isn't really working out, and he says good-bye to Dr. Melfi once and for all. Janice grows impatient with the pace of Bobby's mourning process and decides to accelerate matters by using a Ouija board to demonstrate the unhealthy impact his grief has on the kids. Not long after, they're reheating Karen's last sacred

I'M A MISERABLE PRICK! I'VE SAID IT SINCE DAY ONE.
—TONY SOPRANO

ziti. Tony, Johnny Sack, and Carmine continue to clash over the split on the HUD scam, and the appraiser on the deal takes beatings from both sides. As things heat up, Tony heads to Miami to try to get some resolution from Carmine's son, but he comes back empty-handed. In court Junior's mental incompetency bid is denied, and the trial moves forward.

Season 4, Episode 12:
"ELOISE"

Directed by: James Hayman

Written by: Terence Winter

Season 4, Episode 13:
"WHITECAPS"

Directed by: John Patterson

Written by: Robin Green & Mitchell Burgess and David Chase

Season 5, Episode 1:
"TWO TONYS"

Directed by: Tim Van Patten

Written by: Terence Winter and David Chase

CLOSING ARGUMENTS AT JUNIOR'S trial can only mean one thing: Let the juror intimidation begin. Tony's mistreatment of Carmela is getting to be too much for Furio to take—so much so that he briefly considers rubbing out the boss during a late night of drinking. That's when he knows it's time to skip town. Carmela is devastated, and a traditional tea at the Plaza with Meadow ends bitterly. In an attempt to prove his loyalty to Tony, Paulie raids a little old lady's mattress, but things get complicated and she ends up dead. When payback for roughing up Tony's appraiser leaves Johnny Sack's restaurant trashed, the union is called to the esplanade

WE'VE GONE WAY TOO FAR TO LET IT ALL GO TO SHIT.

—JOHNNY SACK

site, and work comes to a halt. A clandestine meeting between Tony and Johnny Sack reveals Johnny's mounting frustration with his boss and the ongoing feud: "If something were to happen to Carmine, this would go away."

YOU ARE NOT SLEEPING IN MY BED, TONY. THE THOUGHT OF IT NOW MAKES ME SICK.

—CARMELA SOPRANO

ANYTHING'S POSSIBLE WITH FRIENDS in the right places: A deadlocked jury grants Junior his freedom. Tony and Johnny Sack finally reach an agreement on the HUD matter, and Tony goes forward with the hit on Carmine, ordering the newly sober Christopher to take care of it. A last-minute compromise from Carmine finds Tony calling off the job. Things are looking up between Tony and Carmela when he surprises his wife by buying a house at the shore. But Irina, bitter about Tony's influence on her split with Zellman, places a call to the Soprano residence and clues Carmela in on Tony's interlude with Svetlana. This time is the last time, and a furious Carmela kicks Tony out. Tony decamps to the screening room of the Soprano compound, but when another vicious fight prompts Carmela to confess her love for Furio and Tony to react violently, it's clear he's got to leave.

TONY HAS MOVED OUT OF THE HOUSE and a not-so-friendly neighborhood bear visits the Soprano yard in his absence. Reluctant to surrender his role as protector, Tony sends over a young recruit to keep watch. Christopher gets prickly about being the new made guy on the block and the high-priced dinner tabs he's expected to pick up. A plea to Tony brings little sympathy—after all, it's tradition. Thanks to Paulie's "generosity" and healthy appetite, Christopher gets stuck with a $1,200 bill, and when he stiffs the waiter on the tip, he and Paulie suddenly become murder accomplices, and any building tension between the two subsides. Just released from the can, old-school Feech La Manna is ready to get back in the game, but Tony's more interested in getting Dr. Melfi to go out with him. She declines, citing therapeutic reasons, but when Tony persists, she's finally forced to judge him.

Season 5, Episode 2:
"RAT PACK"
Directed by: Alan Taylor
Written by: Matthew Weiner

Season 5, Episode 3:
"WHERE'S JOHNNY?"
Directed by: John Patterson
Written by: Michael Caleo

Season 5, Episode 4:
"ALL HAPPY FAMILIES"
Directed by: Rodrigo Garcia
Written by: Toni Kalem

TONY'S COUSIN TONY BLUNDETTO IS among the crop of those recently out of jail. After fifteen years he has cleaned up his ways and wants to go straight ... as a massage therapist. But Tony B.'s not without attitude, and after he makes some jokes at his cousin's expense, Tony S. makes it clear that's no way to treat the boss. In the wake of Junior's hung jury, the Feds have a hard-on for Tony now

I AM BEIN' RIPPED APART HERE.
—ADRIANA LA CERVA

more than ever, and they've enlisted union rep Jack Massarone to wear a wire to a meeting with him. Tony gets a tip that betrayal's in the air, but it's only when his friend tells Tony it looks like he's lost weight that Tony realizes he's found the rat, and he does some swift exterminating. Carmine Sr. checks out permanently, laying the ground for yet another power struggle.

FEECH LA MANNA SAID HE WANTED back in the action, and he's taking the initiative. After forcibly assuming local yard contractor Sal Vitro's territory, he clashes with Paulie, who has an allegiance to Sal from back in the day. Carmine Sr.'s death has caused some confusion about exactly where earnings should be going, and Johnny Sack enlists Phil Leotardo to make it clear the cash should be kicked to him. As Tony sees it, the best solution is a power-sharing agreement among Sack, Carmine Jr., and Angelo Garepe. Johnny's not convinced. Adriana makes the discovery that her dealings with the FBI might be a long-term commitment. Junior's not quite himself these days, but this time it's for real. After he goes missing for a day, it's determined he has suffered a series of mini strokes, and Tony is forced to forgive the old man for recent offenses he's probably not even aware of.

IT WAS ONLY A MATTER OF TIME. The ongoing turf battle between Johnny Sack and Little Carmine has claimed its first victims: Lorraine Calluzzo and her partner—and Carmine Jr. wants revenge. In Tony's camp, Feech La Manna repeatedly undermines the boss's authority, in part because he can't get used to taking orders from a "kid." Despite efforts to appease Feech, Tony ultimately realizes he can't keep the old man around. Remembering the time Feech forgave him for a youthful transgression, Tony feels merciful, and he arranges for a parole violation to make Feech disappear while still breathing. Back home Carmela's dealing with some issue of disrespect as well, with the increasingly rebellious A.J. When a night in

(EXCITED)
I MIGHT BE LEARNING DISABLED!!
—ANTHONY SOPRANO

the city leaves her son with no eyebrows, she ships him off to live with Tony. A meeting with a counselor at A.J.'s school plants the seeds for Carmela's first affair.

Season 5, Episode 5:
"IRREGULAR AROUND THE MARGINS"

Directed by: Allen Coulter

Written by: Robin Green & Mitchell Burgess

Season 5, Episode 6:
"SENTIMENTAL EDUCATION"

Directed by: Peter Bogdanovich

Written by: Matthew Weiner

Season 5, Episode 7:
"IN CAMELOT"

Directed by: Steve Buscemi

Written by: Terence Winter

ADRIANA'S ANXIETY IS NOW MANI-festing itself physically, in the form of irritable bowel syndrome. She finds herself spending some quality time with Tony at Crazy Horse—bonding, doing coke, and coming dangerously close to kissing. Tony gets kudos from Dr. Melfi for finally resisting a destructive impulse. Even so, Tony is back at the club, and a 2 A.M. drive with Adriana ends with a flipped Escalade and a trip to the hospital. Despite Tony's and Adriana's assertions that nothing happened, word spreads fast on the Mafia grapevine, and Christopher is left enraged at his boss's betrayal. After falling off the wagon with renewed vigor, Christopher pays a visit to the Bing to confront Tony with a bullet. It takes a trip to the emergency room doctor who treated Adriana to assuage Christopher's suspicions. A night out at Vesuvio featuring a surprise appearance by Carmela helps put the rumors to rest.

LIVING WITH DAD SOUNDS A LOT better than it actually is, and A.J. wants back in the Soprano house, where for starters there's food. Tony B. gets an offer from Mr. Kim to partner on a massage business, and

YOU MADE A COMMITMENT TO EACH OTHER BEFORE GOD.

—FATHER PHIL

when he passes his certification exam, renovations go into high gear. But when $12K almost literally falls into Tony B.'s lap, he gets a taste of the mob life again and reverts to his pre-incarceration ways—first by roughing up Kim, and ultimately deciding he's back in with Tony S. Carmela enjoys the thrill of the single life by getting intimately involved with A.J.'s counseler, but the affair goes sour when he accuses her of using him to repair her son's troubles at school. Carmela sees it as guilt by association, but the truth is it's more like guilt through imitation.

JUNIOR'S TAKING HIS MEDICATION, and it appears to be working. His latest scheme is getting out of the house by attending the funerals of anyone even remotely connected to him. At one such gathering, Tony meets Fran, his dad's attractive and charming *goomara*, who regales him with stories of the glamorous good old days. It's not long, however, before Tony sees the less enchanting and parasitic side of his new friend and the destructive impact she had on his father's relationship with his own family. Back in recovery, Christopher gets support from J.T., a screenwriter and fellow former addict. When his new friend catches a buzz

GASSED? MY FATHER TOLD ME THEY TOOK HIM TO A FARM.

—TONY SOPRANO

from high-stakes gambling, he turns to Christopher for a hefty loan, which his renewed taste for heroin prevents him from making good on. Their coffee dates are a thing of the past; now Christopher is stopping by to beat the cash out of him.

Season 5, Episode 8:
"MARCO POLO"

Directed by: John Patterson

Written by: Michael Imperioli

Season 5, Episode 9:
"UNIDENTIFIED BLACK MALES"

Directed by: Tim Van Patten

Written by: Matthew Weiner and Terence Winter

Season 5, Episode 10:
"COLD CUTS"

Directed by: Mike Figgis

Written by: Robin Green & Mitchell Burgess

LITTLE CARMINE HAS MOVED UP north, and he's already working to cement some key alliances with the New York crew. Johnny Sack is determined to retain his men's loyalty, and he demands Tony pay for the damage he inflicted on Phil Leotardo's car. Tony acquiesces, on the condition the work is done at Pussy's old body shop, now run by widow Angie. Carmela plans a seventy-fifth-birthday party for her dad, Hugh, but when she says Tony is not invited, her father refuses to be present if the man of the house isn't there. Tony brings a rare rifle for Hugh, sausage for the grill, and desire for Carmela, who ends up spending the night with him. Tony B. is approached by Carmine's camp about a hit job but turns it down, citing his cousin's edict to not get involved. A financial change of heart finds him pulling the trigger and hobbling away.

WELL, MAYBE HE WANTS TO FUCK ME AND THEN KILL ME!

—FINN DETROLIO

AFTER THE HIT ON JOEY PEEPS, Johnny Sack is convinced Carmine Jr. is responsible. Tony advocates calling a truce before things get out of control and protects Tony B., telling Sack he was with his cousin the night of the murder. Thing is, Tony S. has his own suspicions about Tony B., but his guilt runs deep, and he installs his cousin as the head of a casino. Meadow gets Finn a job at Tony's construction site, and Finn witnesses some mob behavior he finds unsettling. Then he catches Vito in a compromising position—with another man. A blowout fight with Meadow ends with the couple engaged. Carmela's doing her best to go forward with the divorce but finds that nobody will take a case against Tony Soprano. In therapy Tony comes clean about the night long ago when Tony B. got pinched instead of him: A fight with his mother had set off his first panic attack.

THE JOEY PEEPS HIT CONTINUES TO cause strife between Johnny Sack and Tony. The latest shot across the bow is a missing shipment of Vespas, which Tony later learns was picked up by one Phil Leotardo. The sale of the upstate homestead of retired wise guy Pat Blundetto means a trip for Christopher and Tony B., who are recruited by Tony to unearth some bodies on the property. The two bond over grave-digging, griping about their boss, and making jokes at his expense. After a Pee-Wee soccer game scuffle ends with Janice arrested for assault, Bobby demands she enlist in some anger-management classes. Meanwhile, Tony's having some rage issues as well, beating a bartender at the Bing with little cause. Sunday dinner at Janice's shows her classes might actually be working, until Tony antagonizes her with a remark about son Harpo—and she goes after him with a fork.

Season 5, Episode 11:
"THE TEST DREAM"
Directed by: Allen Coulter
Written by: David Chase and Matthew Weiner

Season 5, Episode 12:
"LONG TERM PARKING"
Directed by: Tim Van Patten
Written by: Terence Winter

Season 5, Episode 13:
"ALL DUE RESPECT"
Directed by: John Patterson
Written by: David Chase and Robin Green & Mitchell Burgess

A NIGHT BETWEEN TONY AND VALEN-tina ends with a freak accident that leaves her badly burned. When Phil Leotardo and his brother Billy take out Angelo Garepe, Tony B.'s father figure in jail, Tony's got a very bad feeling. He is escaping his own

> ## THE OBJECT IS TO LEARN WHAT YOU SAW IN ME. NOT WHAT I SAW IN YOU.
> —GLORIA TRILLO (IN TONY'S DREAM)

housekeeper at the Plaza when he gets the news that Tony B. has retaliated by killing Billy. A restless night of sleep brings Tony ominous dreams populated by dead people, Annette Bening, and the recurring question "Is he prepared to do what he needs to?" The only thing that comforts him is an early-morning phone call to Carmela.

AFTER TONY SWEARS OFF ANY FUTURE extramarital activities (and seems open to helping Carmela finance a real-estate venture), the man of the house has moved back in. Tony B., however, is nowhere to be found. A wiretapped phone call from upstate gives Tony a good idea of where he's hiding out, and he's willing to take care of things, but Sack insists Phil be the one to settle matters in his own way. With Little Carmine abdicating his bid for top boss, Johnny's feeling strong-willed. A murder at Crazy Horse lands Adriana back at the Feds' office, but the only way out is to wear a wire or go witness protection. She pitches the program to Christopher, who seems ready to make a change. But when Adriana gets news from Tony that Christopher has attempted suicide, she rushes to his side and meets her death in the woods.

TONY HAS MADE AN UNPOPULAR decision: to protect Tony B. at all costs. His crew isn't happy about it, feeling the boss's resolve has more to do with a war of egos with Johnny Sack than anything related to "family" loyalty. Tony seeks Junior's counsel, but his uncle is too preoccupied with legal troubles. A session with Dr. Melfi reminds Tony that all of his feelings for Tony B. are rooted in guilt. With Tony B. anxiously awaiting a message from Tony at Uncle Pat's farmhouse, Tony goes there and delivers it: a point-blank shot to the forehead. Hoping to finally restore some peace, Tony heads to Johnny Sacks's house. The two rivals settle their differences, just in time for the Feds to flood Johnny's yard and take him into custody. Having fled into the woods, Tony calls his lawyer and learns the cops aren't looking for him. For now.

> ## I'VE KNOWN YOU SINCE YOU WERE A KID, TON'. FRANKLY, YOU GOT A PROBLEM WITH AUTHORITY.
> —SILVIO DANTE

Season 6, Episode 1:
"MEMBERS ONLY"
Directed by: Tim Van Patten
Written by: Terence Winter

Season 6, Episode 2:
"JOIN THE CLUB"
Directed by: David Nutter
Written by: David Chase

Season 6, Episode 3:
"MAYHAM"
Directed by: Jack Bender
Written by: Matthew Weiner

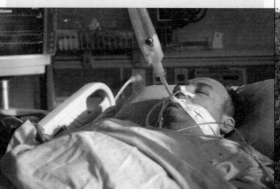

WITH JOHNNY SACK IN JAIL, PHIL Leotardo is the face of the New York crew, and Tony finds his demands increasingly

> **I'M GOING TO GET UNCLE JUNIOR FOR THIS. DON'T WORRY. YOU'RE MY DAD, AND I'M GOING TO PUT A BULLET IN HIS FUCKING MUMMY HEAD, I PROMISE.**
> —ANTHONY JUNIOR

hard to deal with. When one of Phil's guys jumps Hesh and his son-in-law Eli on account of some bad information, relations between the two men become even more strained. Gene Pontecorvo has come into some money and wants to retire to Florida, but when the Feds' main informant, Ray Curto, kicks it, Gene's called in to take his place. He finds a way out, though—with a noose. Uncle Junior is increasingly delusional, and citing family loyalty, Tony refuses to "Green Grove" him. Tony soon learns he might be in over his head in caring for Junior, when in a fit of paranoia his uncle shoots Tony in the stomach.

SOMETHING'S NOT QUITE RIGHT. Tony's wife isn't Carmela, he's staying at a hotel he wouldn't be caught dead in, and he's got the ID and briefcase of Kevin Finnerty, a solar-heating salesman from Arizona. Here's the problem: Tony's in intensive care thanks to Junior's shot to his gut. Things don't look good, and while "Kevin" is being accosted by some Buddhist monks, Carmela keeps a vigil and Silvio takes the reins in Tony's absence. Meanwhile, Junior is in custody, and a psychologist is interviewing him in his diminished capacity. Agent Harris feels out Christopher for any help with his new antiterrorism beat, and A.J., finally at his father's bedside,

> **I'M FORTY-SIX YEARS OLD. I MEAN WHO AM I? WHERE AM I GOING?**
> —TONY SOPRANO

swears revenge on Uncle Junior. He also confides to Carmela that he has flunked out of school. Back in Tony's alternative universe, he's been diagnosed with Alzheimer's.

EVEN WITH THE BOSS ON HIS DEATH-bed, business continues as usual, and a score against some Colombians pulls in a million-dollar payday. Petty politics continue as well: Silvio reluctantly plays boss, sorting out squabbles among the members of the Sopra-no crew. Carmela sees Dr. Melfi at the grocery store and declines her professional help, but when troubles with A.J. drive her to the brink, she goes to the couch. Christopher reconnects with J.T., his screenwriting and gambling-addict friend, and is willing to forgive the deadbeat's debt if he pens Christopher's mafia-themed screenplay. A pitch meeting with potential family investors leaves them skeptical of the idea. Back in Costa Mesa, Tony has arrived at the Finnerty family reunion, but at the hospital he's gone into cardiac arrest. On the Finnerty compound a little girl calls out, "Don't go, Daddy"—and it's then that Tony finally wakes up, with daughter Meadow at his side.

Season 6, Episode 4:

"THE FLESHY PART OF THE THIGH"

Directed by: Alan Taylor

Written by: Diane Frolov & Andrew Schneider

Season 6, Episode 5:

"MR. & MRS. JOHN SACRIMONI REQUEST"

Directed by: Steve Buscemi

Written by: Terence Winter

Season 6, Episode 6:

"LIVE FREE OR DIE"

Directed by: Tim Van Patten

Written by: David Chase & Terence Winter and Robin Green & Mitchell Burgess

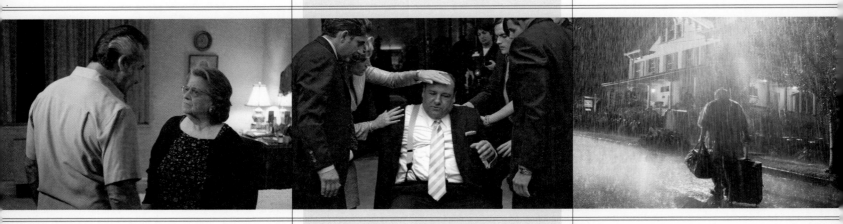

TONY'S ON THE MEND, BUT THERE'S still work to be done. The death of Jason Barone's father finds his son, who's been kept in the dark about his dad's unsavory associates, selling off the sanitation business. Tony relies on the venture for a W-2, insurance, and a healthy cash flow, but his advice to Jason to let him take care of things falls on deaf ears. To complicate matters, Johnny Sack is moving in on the business, setting off some tense negotiations regarding Tony's take going forward. Paulie learns his dying Aunt Dottie is really his mother, so he cuts off ties with duplicitous "mom" Nucci. Bobby helps a rapper boost his career and street cred by offering to shoot him. Some deep conversations between Tony and fellow patient Schwinn leave Tony in a more philosophical state of mind, and he finally agrees to a deal on the Barone split with Sack.

WHEN JOHNNY SACK'S DAUGHTER gets married, Johnny is released for six hours to attend with U.S. Marshals in tow. He takes the opportunity to persuade Tony to take out Rusty Milio, but he leaves sobbing in front of all his guests as the Marshals haul him back to jail. Tony shows some weakness as well,

---

ALLEGRA, ISN'T THAT A COLD MEDICINE?

— CHRISTOPHER MOLTISANTI

---

passing out on his way into the church, but he later reasserts his power by beating up his hefty new bodyguard. Lawyers spar over Junior's mental state while he insists on his innocence, saying Tony's shooting was caused by a gun malfunction. Under the guise of making some collections, Vito heads to a gay bar and is spotted by some fellow wise guys. With gun in hand, he places a panicked call to Silvio at 3 A.M. from a motel, but for now it seems his secret is safe.

WORD OF VITO'S OTHER LIFE HITS the streets, and Tony is pressured to take out his top earner in response. Tony demands some confirmation and thinks maybe Vito deserves a second chance, like the one he just got himself. Carmela finds out real estate isn't so easy: Her spec house gets ransacked, and she can't get Tony to focus on talking to a building inspector. She's also concerned about Angie Bonpensiero, who in becoming a businesswoman seems a little too busy for her friends and a lot less legitimate when it comes to running the body shop. Meadow and Finn once again clash over her father's livelihood, and the hit on Rusty for Johnny Sack moves forward with the enlistment of Corky Caporale. Vito's hiding out in pastoral New Hampshire, but the discord he's causing among the troops back home pushes Tony to make him a marked man.

IT'S 2006, THERE'S PILLOW BITERS IN THE SPECIAL FORCES.

— TONY SOPRANO

Season 6, Episode 7:

"LUXURY LOUNGE"

Directed by: Danny Leiner

Written by: Matthew Weiner

Season 6, Episode 8:

"JOHNNY CAKES"

Directed by: Tim Van Patten

Written by: Diane Frolov &
Andrew Schneider

Season 6, Episode 9:

"THE RIDE"

Directed by: Alan Taylor

Written by: Terence Winter

TONGUES ARE WAGGING THAT ARTIE Bucco's off his culinary game, and raves are coming in for Vesuvio's competition, Da Giovanni's. When Tony attends Phil Leotardo's confirmation lunch for his grandson at the new joint, he feels like a traitor. With business falling off rapidly at Vesuvio, Artie is resistant to any helpful suggestions, and things take a turn for the worse when his new hostess, Martina, teams up with Paulie's man Benny for an Amex scam at the restaurant, which cuts into business even more. It all comes to a boil, and Benny and Artie have it out; Artie's hand ends up scalded in marinara. Christopher jets to L.A. with Carmine to discuss their film project, *Cleaver*, with Ben Kingsley. As the actor gives him the Hollywood runaround, Christopher remembers his penchant for cocaine and hookers and discovers a taste for high-end swag—and satisfies the latter by mugging Lauren Bacall.

SOMETIMES YOU TELL LIES SO LONG, YOU DON'T KNOW WHEN TO STOP.

—VITO SPATAFORE

DRAWN INTO THE NEW YORK CLUB scene, A.J. is trading on his father's reputation, and soon he's requesting that Tony and Carmela subsidize his new player lifestyle. He's flatly denied. A.J. is still holding a grudge against Junior, and when he heads to the hospital with a knife, he's busted and humiliated. Tony is approached by real estate agent Julianna Skiff about selling a neighborhood store, but he refuses, citing the lowball price. A sweeter offer ends up sealing the deal, but Tony can't close one with Julianna because of his new fidelity agreement with Carmela. Vito has adopted the persona of author "Vince" and has taken a liking to diner owner and volunteer firefighter Jim. An initial move by Jim finds Vito rejecting him with force, but it's not long before the two ride off for a romantic picnic.

PAULIE IS CHARGED WITH RUNNING the annual Feast of St. Elzear and makes a few bad decisions. A financial disagreement with the parish priest leaves the saint's statue without its traditional gold hat, and skimping on ride repairs leads to Bobby Bacala's concern for new baby Nica's safety, so he and Paulie clash. At the feast, Carmela sees Adriana's world-weary mother, who shares her suspicions that Christopher is behind her daughter's disappearance. Christopher, meanwhile, has moved on, getting married to pregnant girlfriend Kelli, but he's also getting drunk with Tony after a major wine heist and shooting up with Rusty Milio's killer, Corky. And Paulie's got more troubles than a missing hat—he's had a biopsy for possible prostate cancer and can't get an answer from his doctor on the results. Still running the show for Johnny Sack, Phil Leotardo makes a move to shut out his boss.

Season 6, Episode 10:
"MOE N' JOE"
Directed by: Steve Shill

Written by: Matthew Weiner

Season 6, Episode 11:
"COLD STONES"
Directed by: Tim Van Patten

Written by: Diane Frolov & Andrew Schneider and David Chase

Season 6, Episode 12:
"KAISHA"
Directed by: Alan Taylor

Written by: Terence Winter and David Chase & Matthew Weiner

THE FEDS TALLY UP JOHNNY SACK'S considerable assets for forfeiture in an attempt to get the boss to flip. No dice. Instead,

> ## BEING A RAT—WHERE I'M COMIN' FROM, THAT'S LIKE ASKING A PERSON... TO BECOME A FUCKIN' NAZI.
> — JOHNNY SACK

Sack asks for Tony's help with forcing the sale of a New Orleans equipment-leasing company, but Tony's lukewarm on the idea. After Vito admits to Jim he's not really a writer, the couple move in together, and Vito takes a crack at an honest living. But it's not long before Vito has split town. Janice needles Tony about making Bobby a captain, and while in therapy Tony ruminates on his contentious relationship with her. When he surfaces, he has arranged for the sale of Johnny Sack's house to Janice at a reduced price, in exchange for doing the New Orleans job. And then the news: Johnny has plead guilty, and Phil Leotardo says all bets are off regarding New York–New Jersey agreements.

WITH JOHNNY SACK GONE FOR FIF-teen years, Tony and Phil meet to discuss business, but talks quickly turn sour. Vito's back in Jersey and tracks down Tony to say he wants back in the action in the more tolerant atmosphere of Atlantic City. Tony considers the proposal, but when Phil hears Vito's still around, Tony is forced to order the hit to prevent an all-out war. When Phil's guys get to Vito first, it's a blatant disrespect of Tony's authority, and he's striking back where it hurts Phil most: his bottom line. A.J.continues to cause his parents headaches, getting fired from his Blockbuster job, and Meadow is moving to California to be with Finn. Carmela takes off to Paris with Rosalie Aprile, while Tony seethes to Dr. Melfi about his insolent son. His solution is to make A.J. work construction, a demand he punctuates by shattering the window of A.J.'s car.

> ## IT WAS COMPLICATED. I WAS WORKING THINGS OUT.
> — VITO SPATAFORE

THE NEW YORK–NEW JERSEY WAR rages on. Just as it seems the fallout from the Vito situation is settling, Tony blows up Phil's wire room. Little Carmine is concerned about all the money the conflict is costing, and a sit-down is called. A truce appears imminent until the murder of Phil's brother is brought up, but Phil loses his fighting ways when a coronary lays him up for six months. Carmela hears of Liz La Cerva's attempted suicide, and when she expresses interest in hiring a private investigator to look into Adriana's disappearance, Tony suddenly backs her spec house again. A.J. meets Blanca Selgado at the construction site and the two quickly become involved, even though she's ten years his senior and has a kid. Meanwhile, Christopher has connected with Julianna Skiff through AA and confesses the affair to Tony, because he really doesn't want to tell him he's using again.

PHOTOGRAPHY CREDITS

This book was produced by MELCHER MEDIA, INC.
124 W. 13th Street • New York, NY 10011 • www.melcher.com

Publisher............................CHARLES MELCHER
Associate Publisher........................BONNIE ELDON
Editor in Chief..............................DUNCAN BOCK
Project Editor..................................LIA RONNEN
Assistant Editor..........................LAUREN NATHAN
Production Director....ANDREA HIRSH/KURT ANDREWS

Design................................HEADCASE DESIGN

AUTHOR ACKNOWLEDGMENTS
Thanks to David Chase, Ilene Landress, and the rest of *The
Sopranos* cast and crew, all of whom withstood my hanging
around and asking questions with remarkable patience, insight
and generosity. None of you are quoted here enough, and too
many, for reasons of space, not at all, though your help was
invaluable. This last group includes but is by no means limited
to: Jason Minter, Mark Kamine, Hans Graffunder, Kristen Bern-
stein, April Taylor, Steve Kornacki, Todd Judson, Ginger Gonzalez,
Dared Wright, Charlie Foster, Chris Collins, Anna Lombardo,
Ashley Bearden, Daisy Montfort, Russell Eida, John Spady,
David Moriarty, Craig Blankenhorn, Anthony Baldasare, Eliza-
beth Feldbauer, Louis Zuppardi. The book simply would not
have been completed without the skill, forbearance, and good
company of Jennifer Fistere. Gratitude to the multi-talented Lia
Ronnen, for thinking this could be done in the time allotted and
convincing me that I was the person to do it, and the staff at
Melcher Media. Finally, thanks to Barry Martin, Barbara Martin,
and Scott Martin. And Nicole Keeter.

MELCHER MEDIA ACKNOWLEDGMENTS
Special thanks to David Chase, Ilene Landress, Terence Winter,
Matt Weiner, Andrew Schneider and Diane Frolov.

Thanks to the team at HBO: Chris Albrecht, Carolyn Strauss, Eric
Kessler, Courteney F. Monroe, James Costos, Bree Conover,
Gurmeet Kaur, Tobe Becker, Gina Balian, Victoria Frazier, Jamaal
Lesane, and Stacey Abiraj.

Thanks also to Victoria Alfonso, Jonathan Ambar, David Brown,
Daniel del Valle, Heidi Ernst, Richard Fraiman, Sarah Gainer,
Peter Harper, Mimi O'Connor, Carol Pittard, Alessandra Raffer-
ty, Holly Rothman, Nathan Sayers, Lindsey Stanberry, Alex
Tart, Shoshana Thaler, Betty Wong, and Megan Worman.

HEADCASE DESIGN would like to thank Jessica Hische
for her design and production help.

ABOUT THE AUTHOR
BRETT MARTIN has been a frequent contributor to *Van-
ity Fair, GQ, The New York Times*, and many other publications,
as well as to public radio's "This American Life." He lives in
Brooklyn, New York.

ABOUT THE DESIGNERS
PAUL KEPPLE and JUDE BUFFUM are better known
as HEADCASE DESIGN, an award-winning graphic design
and illustration studio based in Philadelphia. Their work has been
recognized by such publications as the *AIGA's 365* and *50 Books/50
Covers, American Illustration, Communication Arts*, and *Print*.